FEEDING FRENZY!

THE WILD NEW WORLD OF THE SAN JOSE SHARKS

STEVE CAMERON

Taylor Publishing Company
   Jack Smith   *Publisher, Director, Fine Books*
   Bob Snodgrass   *Publishing Consultant*
TD Media
   Tony Seidl   *Packaging*
   Frank Coffey   *Consulting Editor*
Robert Engle Design   *Design and Art Direction*

Photo Editor   Rocky Widner
Fiber Optic Photo   Wolf Photography and Chris Dennis
Dust Jacket Design   Mike Stromberg
Contributing Photographers   Chris Dennis, Rocky Widner,
                               Chris Vleisides, Dan Hamilton, Don Smith.

Contributing Artists   Michele Bohbot   page i
                             Charles Schulz   page 153

Contributing Artists–Gatefold   Mike Blatt   Sharks-head tunnel
                             Anatoly Paseka   22nd Century Players
                             Mark Ericksen   Shark breaking through ice

Sharks Logo Design   Terry Smith / JRS Enterprises
Sharks Logotype Designs   Mike Blatt
Sharks Ticket Series Design   Stratford Design
Select photos courtesy AP Worldwide Photos, Canapress Photo Service
Remaining photos courtesy the San Jose Sharks

Copyright © 1994 by Steve Cameron, Taylor Publishing Company and the San Jose Sharks

Published by Taylor Publishing Company,
Dallas, Texas

ISBN: 0-87833-102-6 (General)
ISBN: 0-87833-103-4 (Limited)
ISBN: 0-87833-104-2 (Collectors)

fb
TAYLOR

For everyone back home
who wondered what became of me.

About the Author

Steve Cameron has been covering hockey and assorted other sports as a newspaper reporter and columnist for more than two decades. Winner of numerous awards for overall sports writing and works on subjects as varied as greyhound racing and basketball on the Navajo reservation, Cameron also edited a golf guide to the Caribbean which was published in 1983.

Cameron is the author of six sports-oriented books, including commemoratives on the Green Bay Packers, Portland Trail Blazers and *Last of a Breed*, a biography of baseball legend George Brett. Cameron's account of a cross-country rail trip, *Last Train to America*, will be released by Taylor Publishing Company in 1995.

Now a full-time author and radio commentator, Cameron grew up in the Bay Area and currently resides in Kansas City.

Table of Contents

ACKNOWLEDGEMENTS

This book originated at a specific place and time—about six inches in front of my living-room TV set, just a few seconds after I tried to reach through the screen and re-direct Johan Garpenlov's slap shot in Game Six of the playoffs.

The Sharks' story already had become remarkable enough that millions of people were shopping for teal underwear and teal dental floss, but somehow, that playoff saga seemed to push things to another level entirely.

The team, the town, the turnaround—hey, it was obvious: What we needed here were words, pictures and a nice hard cover. A real live book, like the ones you can find down at the mall.

Authors and publishers, though, would be more than happy to tell you that it's one bucket of hockey pucks just sitting around and chatting up some nifty book project, and quite another actually making the vision come to life.

And so it was with *Feeding Frenzy!*

It's customary for an author to acknowledge that he or she couldn't have done it alone. In the case of this book you happen to be holding—given the time frame involved and everyone's determination that we wouldn't settle for some tacky-looking, hurry-up-and-keep-it-simple rehash—saying thanks to the folks who made it happen just barely scratches the surface.

Everyone in the Sharks organization was unbelievably cooperative, beginning with our main man, Matt Levine, who approved the project in the first place and then used his considerable talents and influence to keep things rolling. Not only that, Matt gave each of us a bottle of S.J. Sharkie's chardonnay—is he a prince or what?

Herb Briggin was a huge help breaking logjams along the way, and Paul Turner from the Media Relations department proved he could find clippings or reference on <u>anything</u> at a moment's notice. Paul also set a one-day record by tying up our fax machine from dawn 'til closing when we requested background material on the 1993-94 season.

Club owner George Gund not only called in from his plane and then from a hockey rink in rural Minnesota just to answer a few questions, he also provided some pictures from scouting junkets to far-flung spots. Sharks execs Art Savage, Greg Jamison, Frank Jirik, Dean Lombardi and Chuck Grillo all took time to retell the story just once more, and so did coach Kevin Constantine—which, considering how tightly he schedules his days, perhaps was the great coup of all.

Thanks to Rocky Widner, who shuffled through thousands of his Sharks photos to find the ones we needed—and then went out searching for specific shots we might want to acquire from somewhere else. This book belongs to Rocky and his spectacular artwork as much as it does to me.

Quite a few people in the San Jose area were not only friendly but helpful and made things easier for me personally. Tom McEnery heads the list, and if anyone wants to say that I'm biased because we're both Bellarmine grads, well, they've probably got a case.

Mayor Susan Hammer worked hard to make herself available, and so did people like advertising executive Peter Carter and Chamber of Commerce president Steve Tedesco. But everyone in San Jose—from waitresses in downtown coffee houses to security guards at The Tank—seemed genuinely friendly and more than willing to help.

Quite a bit of material here was gleaned from Bay Area newpapers—stories and columns too numerous to mention individually. But I should give a special nod to several local columnists and reporters who made me smile and filled in a lot of blanks: Mark Purdy, Bud Geracie, Ann Killion, Scott Ostler, Steve Kettmann, Dave Newhouse and of course, that wordsmith from another galaxy, Ray Ratto. I wouldn't trade my box of Ratto clippings for Pavel Bure, even up.

I need to mention some folks back in my adopted home, too. The very first person to hear our ideas for this project was Jim Loria of the Kansas City Blades. Loria was supportive and pointed us toward Levine, and then it was into the fast lane. So as it turns out, the Blades—Loria, Bob Kaser, GM Doug Soetaert, owner Russ Parker—have given Sharks fans more than just promising young hockey players. They've also helped toss this book into the mix.

Thanks as usual to the movers and shakers from Taylor Publishing Company—Arnie Hanson, Jack Smith and Bob Snodgrass. It seems like we've done this dance quite a few times now, but the music still sounds good.

And once again, everyone at TD Media in New York spun some tight circles working on deadline. Frank Coffey, Tony Seidl, John Holms and the staff of Robert Engle Design have earned my gratitude. In particular, Dr. Coffey is very good at talking me down off the ledge when it seems there's just too much to cover and too little time.

Back at the office, Jamie Montgomery and Kim Shannon have taken a lot of calls and tried to explain my whereabouts when I couldn't do it myself.

I can't forget my personal support group, either. Anyone who writes for a living will tell you that close friends, family, confidants—people whose shoulders you can weep on—often keep a project going when the person at the keyboard would otherwise just freeze up like an engine left out overnight in downtown Whitehorse. My own gang includes my sister Kris and her husband Frank Dunn, Cheesehead Jeff Flanagan, radio partner and fellow chocolate chip cookie aficionado Gib Twyman, Melanie Esterline, Tim (Bet the Favorite) Keithley, Tom Jurich and Mike Patrick back out in mountain country—and of course that wonderful voice on the other end of those midnight conversations, Miss Teacher Lady, Beckie Rathke.

I think I'm finally getting the hang of this author routine, and what I know for sure about it is that without everyone else to prop you up, well, you're an empty net and that's Gretzky skating in alone.

For everyone who's keeping me afloat, what do you say we do some more of these book things once we're out of therapy?

—S.C.

INTRODUCTION BY GEORGE GUND

When I started to play hockey as a boy, I was drawn to the game's speed, the sense of freedom and power as I skated up ice and the challenge it was to be creative when handling a stick, managing the puck and manuevering in traffic. Even the sound of my skates and the wind whistling around me as I burst down the ice was like music. The body contact reminded me that this game was about territory as well as artistry.

Ever since then, hockey has been my passion. Originally, I displayed it as a player, then as a coach, and as a participant in developing a junior, senior, and women's program at a grass roots level where no hockey had existed before in Sun Valley, Idaho. Eventually, I demonstrated my love for the game by helping young players develop their skills (through the U.S. Amateur Hockey program) and even break into the National Hockey League.

The latter began with a "minority" interest in the California Golden Seals, some twenty years ago, then ownership of the Cleveland Barons, and Minnesota North Stars with my brother, Gordon.

It's exciting in the '90's to be an owner of a team in the National Hockey League and to know that I share the same passion for the game as our management team, coach, support staff, and players. Hockey is much more to me than a business venture.

But nothing among my avocations or business interests today can compare to the pride I have in the rapid evolution of the San Jose Sharks from the germ of an idea five years ago to becoming one of the most prominent and respected professional sports franchises in the world.

Here in the region I have called my home for more than three decades we have been embraced by the City of San Jose, the Silicon Valley, the Bay Area, all of Northern California...and beyond, across America, Europe and Asia, even Latin America. We have positively influenced the world's perception of the game of hockey, the National Hockey League, the City of San Jose, and how a franchise can reach to the grass roots of its community.

We have done this with a combination of innovative management and leadership, on-ice development and performance and enlightened operation of the San Jose Arena.

But none of the above would have happened without the unwavering support and devotion shown—by you, the "Finatical Fans!" As you enjoy *Feeding Frenzy! The Wild New World of the San Jose Sharks,* listen for the music.

George Gund III
Owner
San Jose Sharks

Foreword
by Ronnie Lott

Whenever people ask me why I'm such a big Sharks fan, and a season-ticket holder since Day One, I tell them it's "unity" in the word, "community."

The same is true for the city of San Jose. One of the first things I discovered when I moved here in 1981, is that this is not a city where you're going to have just a few people be part of something. Everybody wants to be part of everything that's happening. It's always a community effort.

And there was a unity in the community, giving every ounce of our energy into every Sharks game.

It reminded me a lot of when I came to the 49ers in 1981, the first year we won the Super Bowl. We were just this scrapping bunch of young guys, and for some reason we got into this unbelievable mode and the fans got into this unbelievable mode, and here we were going to the Super Bowl.

It was the greatest feeling when you saw how the people rallied behind us.

I had the same feeling sitting in the stands for Sharks games that I did as a player for the Niners. The intensity that moved back and forth from the fans to the players, everything that was happening out there...the players could feel it, they could touch it. It was like the whole stadium was moving on another level. And the team played like that.

Everybody in the city got into it. You had all kinds of people fighting about it, talking about it, thinking about it. It was an amazing thing watching it all unfold. Niners games were like that. Sharks games are like that, too.

I guess a lot people might be surprised that an old football player like myself would get that much into hockey, but I've actually liked it since I was a little kid back in Washington, D.C. We lived in an apartment in Coral Hills, Md., a suburb of D.C., and I'd watch Washington Capitals games on the UHF station on TV. The Capitals were pretty horrible and the other sports were more popular in the D.C. area. Plus, I didn't know much about hockey. But I'd sit there and watch it for hours because it was quick and fast, with lots of action.

When I played football for U.S.C. from '77 to '81, I became a Kings fan. I never had the money for tickets, but again there was the almighty television and I followed a lot of the Kings games.

The great thing about the sport to me is that there is something for everybody at a hockey game. The thing I identify with most is the hitting. I guess that's natural as a football player. But, there's so much more to appreciate in hockey. Whether it's seeing someone take it all the way, one-on-one, or seeing somebody get checked into the boards, or watching someone defend the goal..it's a little bit of every type of action. Everything in all the other sports is combined right there for you in hockey.

When I got back last year, after playing with the Jets in New York, the first thing I wanted to do when I hit San Jose was go to a Sharks game. You heard about the arena, you heard about the excitement, and I had not been to a game at the Shark Tank yet. It was the happening thing to do when I got back. My friends in New York would be talking about the Rangers and all the excitement they generated, and I'd say, 'Hey, we've got that same type of excitement in the Bay.'

After all the traveling last year, I got to maybe the last quarter of the season, about 15 to 20 games. I went a lot with my wife, Karen. It was so funny because the first time I went, I asked, "You want to go?" And she said, "Yeah, I guess." And I said, "Are you sure you'll like it?" "No problem," she said. "I think I'll like it." And from then on it got to the point, 'We can't miss the game, we can't miss the game.' She became a big fan and really got into it.

Watching people like Mayor Susan Hammer and Frank Taylor, who headed the redevelopment of downtown San Jose, has been tremendous. They've got all the citizens of San Jose involved, helped them get a sense of responsibility and pride in our community.

Now you see the excitement generated downtown by Sharks games. You can pop down for a nice meal, then hop over to the arena. It's given some people an opportunity for the first time to really see what downtown San Jose is all about. And you see the economic impact the team has made on the city. I've been part-owner of a restaurant, the Sports City Cafe, the last 2 1/2 years, and you see the people crammed in there before Sharks games.

That's not some spread sheet or pie chart talking about the economic side of hockey here. That's a part-owner in a restaurant seeing it for himself, first-hand.

Put it this way. You can definitely tell when there's a Sharks game. There's nothing but teal downtown. No doubt about it. Teal's become my favorite color.

Ronnie Lott vs.
The Children of
Eastfield Ming Quong
Children's Center

PREFACE

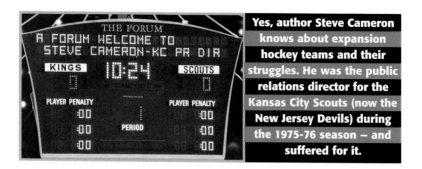

Yes, author Steve Cameron knows about expansion hockey teams and their struggles. He was the public relations director for the Kansas City Scouts (now the New Jersey Devils) during the 1975-76 season — and suffered for it.

Perhaps there is still an imprint of a roast beef sandwich on the wall of the Kemper Arena press box in Kansas City.

I hope so.

Remnants from lingering lunchmeat would serve as perfect testimony to just how extraordinarily difficult a challenge it is turning a National Hockey League expansion team into something that doesn't keep franchise executives lying awake with night sweats.

And that's why this book about the incredible success of the San Jose Sharks through just three seasons of NHL existence makes me smile so often.

Let's scoot back almost two decades. I was working as a sportswriter for the *Topeka* (KANSAS) *Capital-Journal* when Kansas City was awarded an NHL expansion franchise for the 1974-75 season. But hockey hit me like a slap shot from point-blank range.

I fell in love with the game, and I remember the exact time and place. This new team of castoffs, no-hopers, rejects and callow kids—the Kansas City Scouts—set up training camp that first year in Port Huron, Mich. And so off I went to learn about hockey and profile the Scouts for our readers back home.

Please understand that I didn't have your standard credentials as a hockey expert. Yes, I grew up in the San Francisco Bay Area, too, and went to high school at Bellarmine Prep in San Jose. Like so many Sharks fans when that magical team arrived quite recently and began capturing hearts, I had to learn hockey almost from the skates up.

But one afternoon during a scrimmage in Port Huron—the arena, like the town itself, was dark and dreary—the team's PR guy walked me down to a spot behind the glass and just to the side of goalie Michel Plasse. The whole thing amazed me. The speed, the collisions, the remarkable stick-handling skills. And especially the shooting. Blast after blast either thudded off some part of Plasse's anatomy or crashed into the glass in front of us. I flinched every time.

It was phenomenal. I was hooked.

The Scouts went on to plod through the predictable first-year malaise, winning a few exciting games they shouldn't have but generally playing the role of cannon fodder for the NHL's glamour boys. Still, I couldn't get enough.

Thus when one of the Scouts' vice presidents approached me at the start of the next season and asked if I'd be interested in taking over the club's public relations department, I jumped. Irrationally, as it turned out, but this was more like teenage puppy love than any carefully thought out career decision.

In some ways, my lone year in the NHL was one of the best of my life. I don't even need to look back into the media guide to tell you the Scouts were a respectable 11-21-4 at one point—in those days, expansion teams (Washington was the other one) got nothing from the league in terms of talent. But it seemed like we were decent at least. We packed Kemper one night and upset mighty Montreal, and it seemed to me that the Stanley Cup itself couldn't be any better.

There were other joys, as well. My assistants, Chuckie O'Brien and Sandy Wright, were innovative to say the least. We created a neat press dining lounge—music, candles on tables, the whole works—out of a bare storeroom at Kemper. No kidding. Our little PR staff had to set up that room and break it down again for every game. Arena custodians used the place to stack boxes most days. We also became, as far as I know, the first American-based NHL team to provide pregame press notes in both English and French when the Canadiens were in town (Quebec hadn't joined the league yet).

Oh, it was fun.

And then the bottom fell out. What I hadn't checked too thoroughly when I leaped into the PR job was how well the Scouts franchise was being run at the top. In fact, it was chaos. The general partner and his cronies not only botched almost every decision, they began to cut off the flow of money—for staff, for travel expenses, for player movement and acquisition, for everything.

Coach Bep Guidolin quit in January of 1976 and general manager Sid Abel would have if he hadn't owned a small piece of the club. On the ice, we slid from being an interesting spoiler team with a promising future—built around decent players like Wilf Paiement, Simon Nolet, Guy Charron and goalie Denis Herron—to a no-chance gang of minimum-wage ham-and-eggers.

That was hell. It felt like, well, it probably felt a lot like the Sharks' 11-win torture of 1992-93.

Anyhow, my Scouts were doomed and in fact, the franchise went bust the day after the season ended and was shipped off to Colorado—where it failed again before moving to New Jersey. Before our run in Kansas City played itself out, though, we wrapped up that 1975-76 season with an NHL-record, 23-game winless streak. Our record after mid-January was 1-44-8—and just to epitomize the frustration, we had third-period leads in all eight of those ties.

Which brings us to the roast beef sandwich. The incident occurred during the 23-game nightmare, in a match against the Los Angeles Kings. For whatever reason, Kings goalie Rogie Vachon was a sieve that night, and we jumped out to a 4-1 lead in the first period.

It looked like the streak was over, but of course, the Kings quickly got a goal back to make it 4-2. Still, we were getting scoring chances, the surprisingly large crowd at Kemper was into it—hockey fans can rouse you like nobody else—and most of us truly believed our night of deliverance was at hand.

Now picture this situation: We're up 4-2, there are exactly four seconds left in the first period and the Kings get a face-off in the circle to the right of Herron. I remember thinking: Please win this face-off. No flukes here. Please no flukes.

And we did win the draw. The puck was pulled cleanly back to one of our defensemen. Did I say the play started with four seconds remaining? Well, would you believe the Kings scored anyway?

It's true. For whatever reason, our guy mindlessly tried to throw the puck out of the zone—he easily could have eaten the damn thing for lunch as the buzzer sounded—and one of the Kings out at the point had just enough time (our clock operator was as slow as our forwards) to knock this funny-looking knuckleball through a huge crowd of players and past the screened Herron just before the green light went on.

I snapped. I've never reacted to a sports play like that before or since. Talk about unprofessional: I picked up a sandwich (roast beef and swiss) from a tray that had been delivered to the press area for between-period snacks, and whipped the thing across the room—right over the heads of startled reporters and <u>splat</u> against the north wall.

Later, obviously, I was humiliated. But after the game, which naturally we stumbled on to lose, I told Sid Abel about my embarrassment and he said, "If you live to be a thousand years old, you'll never see a team give up another goal that stupid. If I'd had a gun, I'd have shot myself."

Which didn't make me feel so bad about just heaving a sandwich.

That whole sorry tale serves as backdrop for this book, and the enthusiasm I've had for the project since the Sharks and San Jose began going crazy in the spring of 1994.

Here was an expansion team living the dream, and doing it back in the very city where I grew up. Not only that, but I'd already formed another Sharks connection—having seen several key players performing splendidly for the club's International Hockey League affiliate back in Kansas City. Yes, I saw Arturs Irbe long before most of his worshippers in San Jose.

And Kevin Constantine, too.

I can honestly say that watching Kevin's Blades win the IHL Turner Cup one season and then come close the next year without anything close to the talent needed for the task convinced me that this man was destined to be an outstanding NHL coach. A lot of other people who know hockey better than I do clearly saw the same thing, but at least I can claim I watched it all happening.

In fact, at the beginning of the 1993-94 season, I went to a Blades game with good buddy Jeff Flanagan, a reporter from the *Kansas City Star*. Afterwards, we were hanging around general manager Doug Soetaert's office and there were newspaper clips from the Bay Area floating all over

The Sharks and Kansas City do have some extremely happy ties. Sandis Ozolinsh (4) broke into professional hockey with the Blades in 1991-92, the year Kansas City —with Kevin Constantine behind the bench —won the Turner Cup. Team captain Gary Emmons (next page), who later played briefly in San Jose during their 1993-94 turnaround season, hoisted the Cup in '92.

the place. The Sharks were in the midst of their 0-8-1 start and the California media sounded grumbling and doubtful.

Plain as day, I recall Flanagan and I looking at each other and saying something like, "Just wait. They don't know Kevin yet." We couldn't have dreamed of the Stanley Cup conference semifinals, not then, but Kevin Constantine's teams just don't go oh-and-anything, and we knew it before a lot of folks out in San Jose.

So that's the personal side of this book, and why it's such fun to see so many wonderful goals fulfilled.

Some explanation is necessary as well, I think, about how "Feeding Frenzy!" was put together and why it's structured as it is. You'll certainly notice that the Sharks story isn't told in strict chronological order—you know, from awarding of the franchise to picking the name to the expansion draft, etc. I've tried to tell the story the way Sharks fans might yak about it among themselves.

The fairy-tale run of 1994 was the only logical place to start, touching on all the craziness and giddy goings-on that shook San Jose and the Bay Area as the Sharks took off for unimagined heights.

From there, I've tried to go back and explain just what was required for San Jose to get its team and arena in the first place, picking up the on-ice story with cursory nods to those couple of seasons in the Cow Palace—then how Constantine and the whole new cast of characters changed the franchise so dramatically in just one year.

There's a chapter called "The World's Team," which is about two amazing things going on simultaneously—the Sharks' incredible marketing success, which was a smash from Day One, and how and why this team has done so well blending in players from so many countries.

And finally, there is a peek toward the future, which looks so bright for this well-run organization and for revitalized San Jose, a city I once thought did little more than sleep peacefully in the Valley sunshine.

It's a great yarn, and I hope I've done it some justice. Surely most Sharks fans will miss certain plays, favorite games, personal heroes whom they think should have been featured a little more heavily. We all see things through our own eyes, and the nature of books is that the authors get first priority. But that doesn't mean I've gotten it all, or even put things in the same order you might.

But that's OK. There are plenty of memories to go around already, and everything I've seen of the San Jose Sharks indicates there will be many more to come—for the team and the city.

If the Sharks suffer a little setback here and there, which is simply the nature of professional sports, keep the faith. You've got a great thing going.

Just keep a firm grip on that roast beef sandwich.

—Steve Cameron
  San Jose, California
  September 1994

Hello, Lord Stanley

Thonk!

Toronto goalie Felix Potvin heard the sound just a split-second after flailing at air with his blocking pad. "You know the puck is behind you and all you can do is wait for the reaction of the crowd," Potvin said. "The noise tells you what happened."

What Potvin's ears caught was the unmistakable clunk of Johan Garpenlov's whistling slap shot crashing into the crossbar. Then came an audible gasp followed by a collective sigh of relief from the sellout crowd at Maple Leaf Gardens.

Garpenlov's blast —72 seconds into overtime, game six of the NHL's Western Conference semifinals—had indeed slammed squarely into the pipe behind Potvin and ricocheted away. And so by that tiniest margin—say, half an inch—the San Jose Sharks missed clinching the series that would have sent them into a conference

championship matchup against Vancouver.

"I had a look from right in front and got off a good shot," Garpenlov said of the rocket that might have prolonged the Sharks' improbable Cinderella run toward the Stanley Cup finals. "I knew it was going to be close. Sometimes you just don't get the bounce."

Shark coach Kevin Constantine remembered thinking, in that eye-blink of a moment, that perhaps Garpenlov had won the series. But Constantine conceded he had a bad angle on the shot from behind the Sharks' bench and that, frankly, it had all happened so fast, there was wasn't even time to have his hopes lifted and then dashed. Sharks owner George Gund, though, recalled thinking—even in the heartbeat between Garpenlov unloading and the sound of puck meeting iron— that the deed had been done. "I knew it was by Potvin and I really thought it was going in," Gund said. "I really did."

The echo was destined to linger.

"The sound of that crossbar, I'll be hearing it for a long, long time," said veteran center Igor Larionov, the Russian star who had experienced so many thrills at the game's highest levels. "We had a shot at the Cup. We really did."

Oh, the Sharks had other chances in Game Six after Garpenlov's shot. Sandis Ozolinsh couldn't quite pull the trigger on a scoring opportunity a few minutes later and, even after the Leafs got a scruffy-looking goal by Mike Gartner to win the thing 3-2 at 8:38 of overtime, there was still a seventh game.

But the hard-nosed, battle-tested Leafs won that one 4-2—despite being out-shot—and thus the Sharks' inspiring play-off dash was over. Their implausible hope of bathing the Stanley Cup in a teal spotlight had ended, at least for 1994.

Now here's something that most so-called hockey experts, the ones who believed San Jose somehow slipped into postseason play on a pass, might have found surprising about the Sharks' combative departure from the playoffs: The finish was painful.

Proud and defiant as they'd been while dispatching the heavily favored Detroit Red Wings in the first round, as resilient as they'd proven themselves against Toronto, the Sharks were wounded deeply when it was over. By April, the Sharks believed that they could whip anyone.

> "I am crying for this team. I am sad. What we had this year was the best team I've ever been on. Great friends, great chemistry. I wouldn't trade that for a Stanley Cup. Never. That's just how proud I am."
>
> —Arturs Irbe

They cried, these rugged professionals who had stood up to nearly every challenge in what most hockey experts considered nothing less than a miracle season. "Maybe we can feel good about what we accomplished later, maybe we can have a smile or two on the flight home," said winger Ulf Dahlen, whose eyes were rimmed bright red shortly after the final loss to Toronto. "But right now…"

Tough Bob Errey, the Sharks' captain and winner of two Stanley Cup rings with the Pittsburgh Penguins, was crushed, and admitted it. "Guys are really upset," forward Jeff Odgers said. "Our captain—our heart and soul—he's taking it as hard as anybody. Bob has played 12, 13 years. He might be thinking there's not too many more kicks of the can for him, not many more chances to win it."

Center Todd Elik, who had talked openly about his dream of carrying the Cup, made no secret of how hard the disappointment struck everyone in the Sharks locker room.

Goalie Arturs Irbe was as frustrated as any of his teammates, but he was also eloquent in defeat, and addressed just how special these Sharks had become—especially to each other. "I am crying for this team," he said. "I am sad. What we had this year was the best team I've ever been on. Great friends, great chemistry. I wouldn't trade that for a Stanley Cup. Never. That's just how proud I am."

Defenseman Jayson More, one of the Sharks cornerstones, made it clear he appreciated San Jose's support when he told reporters that crowd noise in The Tank was the loudest in the NHL.

"That's a damn good hockey club. They just wouldn't die."

—Pat Burns,
Toronto coach

The effect of knocking out the Red Wings on hostile ice, of Garpenlov's near-miss, of going out at the hands of the Leafs in seven fiercely fought games, was remarkable in so many ways. For one thing, it was obvious these Sharks had long since passed the point of being giddy just to participate in the playoffs. They'd already junked any notion of merely being respectable in hockey's toughest crucible.

"Our goal wasn't just to be competitive or anything like that," defenseman Jeff Norton said. "We knew what we had in our locker room, and our goal was to win the Cup. We'll let other people say we had a good season or a good run in the playoffs. We wanted more than that."

In fact, though it took awhile to sink in for almost everyone outside the Sharks immediate family, these guys actually had been planning to win Lord Stanley's cup—just as coach Constantine instructed them way back in training camp, when such a thought was considered laughable.

The San Jose Sharks, for heaven's sake?

Think about that: The Sharks actually got to a point—in a few short months—where they were crushed by losing a playoff series.

This was a team that won just 11 games in a 1992-93 season that left the rest of the NHL jokingly calling them "Sad Jose," a team that even early in its wondrous turn-around season had gone 0-8-1 and been described by a San Francisco reporter as having a "pathetic persona."

These same Sharks came so far, so fast, that by season's end, they were disconsolate about losing a seven-game series in the Stanley Cup Western Conference semifinals. It was enough to make even the craziest fan dizzy. A team that quite recently was playing in a rodeo arena and counting victories more or less as monthly occurrences suddenly had flashed some serious jaws.

They stormed down the stretch in the regular season playing just about as well as anyone in the league, and ripped off a nine-game unbeaten streak in March and April en route to clinching their first playoff berth. They not only weren't a joke anymore, they had become a downright terrifying opponent—especially in the overheated atmosphere of the playoffs. Just ask the Red Wings, the conference's No. 1 seed, who were booed off their home ice after losing Game Seven 3-2 to the poised, patient Sharks.

Or you might ring up Toronto coach Pat Burns, who kept trying to tell Leafs fans that the Sharks would be a serious pain in the backside. When Toronto survived that hair-raising finish in Game Six, Burns said, "Want to feel my armpits? Even our hockey sticks are sweating." And when the series finally had been won, Burns snapped at reporters who even hinted at the idea that San Jose should have been dispatched a bit more easily.

"That's a damn good hockey club," Burns hissed. "They just wouldn't die."

Yes, these were the once-helpless Sharks he was talking about, and almost no one could have believed it as recently as the autumn of 1993.

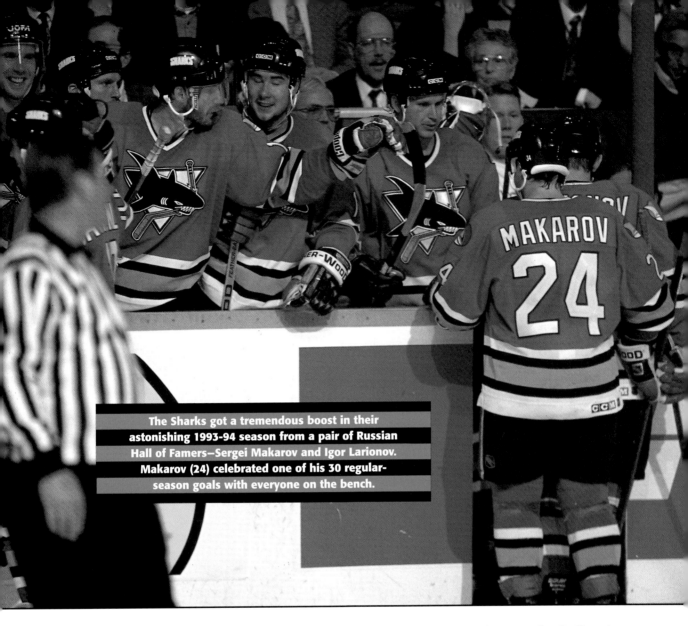

The Sharks got a tremendous boost in their astonishing 1993-94 season from a pair of Russian Hall of Famers—Sergei Makarov and Igor Larionov. Makarov (24) celebrated one of his 30 regular-season goals with everyone on the bench.

San Jose as the darling of the National Hockey League?

Kids with hockey sticks around the world all decked out in teal? The sparkling new arena becoming a centerpiece for civic madness? As many as 40,000 kids in and around the sun-splashed Santa Clara Valley signing up for street hockey through the Sharks & Parks program? Return to glory for Larionov and Sergei Makarov, those former Soviet superstars who somehow recaptured their magnificent on-ice magic?

No, wait a minute: If you want to know how far the Sharks really progressed in 1993-94 and what an impact they had on the sports landscape in North America and elsewhere, consider that they actually converted grumpy Don Cherry. The bellowing TV bard and staunch defender of Canadian hockey—usually to the exclusion of anything else—probably stunned his north-of-the-border audience by conceding that the multinational Sharks were better than he realized. "I can't find it in me to hate 'em," Cherry groused. "Maybe it's the teal. But you know what? These Russians and Latvians really are pretty good."

In their breakthrough season, the Sharks swept a three-game series from the Chicago Black Hawks, all but insured a playoff spot by going 3-0-1 on a brutal March road trip to Pittsburgh, Toronto, Winnipeg and St. Louis, clinched their postseason berth in Los Angeles—where

Young Sharks (goalie Arturs Irbe) and tough veterans like captain Bob Errey tried to fight off the Leafs, including the onrushing Jamie Macoun (34).

As surprising and even heroic as the Sharks' playoff run might have been, the team was distraught when Toronto escaped with a victory in the seventh game of the Western Conference semfinals. Sandis Ozolinsh (6) and the rest of his team- mates rushed to console goalie Arturs Irbe when the long battle finally was over.

The Sharks proved they could dish it out as well as take it in the playoffs, as burly Shawn Cronin (44) demonstrated to Detroit's Keith Primeau.

they'd never won—and generally tossed all previous theories about Team Teal into the trashbin reserved for broken hockey sticks.

And of course, they ignited a love affair back home.

The Sharks became trendy, popular, even fascinating to hockey buffs around the world, but in San Jose, well, the frenzy was almost beyond description. Tom McEnery, the former mayor who risked his political life campaigning for a downtown arena in 1988, put the whole wild success story into this heady perspective: "The Sharks have had a greater impact on San Jose than anything except Silicon Valley. And you could probably get an argument about that on game nights."

Big-city newspapers, TV crews and national magazines galloped into the Santa Clara Valley. Irbe and Ozolinsh, who represented the Sharks grandly at the 1994 NHL All-Star Game in New York, were profiled in *Sports Illustrated* and interviewed by a San Francisco newspaper in their native Latvian tongue. Sharks players were painted on municipal buses in San Jose. Teal paraphernalia became so hot that a gang of thieves broke into the arena shop and made off with team merchandise instead of money. One daring young lady began a fascinating local tradition by hurling her brassiere onto the ice whenever one of the Sharks recorded a hat trick.

The place went nuts.

"Our city is having the time of its life," said Steve Tedesco of the Chamber of Commerce. "This is our team, not San Francisco's team or Oakland's team. All this excitement happened right in the middle of San Jose, so how could we not go crazy over it?"

San Jose Arena became The Shark Tank—famous almost overnight for creative signs, a sea of teal, outrageous costumes, those two Zamboni with fins on top, the blare of that foghorn whenever the Townies scored a goal and an unrelenting racket that sometimes made witnesses feel they might as well be standing on the deck of an aircraft carrier at flight time.

"Our fans are so loud it's just unbelievable," defenseman Jayson More said. "There isn't a building in the league with more noise than this. They just lift us up whenever we need it."

By Stanley Cup time, was there anyone left in the Bay Area who wasn't doing The Chomp in public without fear of being laughed at? Not likely. "I really believe that our fans deserved the success more than we did," Irbe said. "They made us so proud to be playing for the San Jose Sharks."

Larionov has played on Olympic and world championship teams in the former Soviet Union, so you'd figure he'd seen just about everything. But when Igor heard the reaction each time he and his mates skated out of that giant shark's mouth just before game time at The Tank, he was stirred. "You get, what is it called, goosebumps," Larionov said.

Even George Gund, a lifetime optimist who believed all along that hockey could catch fire in the Bay Area, admitted he was amazed by the mania. "I thought something really good could happen," Gund said, "but not nearly so quickly, or with such passion. It was so sudden, and so intense. I've been involved in hockey just about all my life, but this was the best year I've ever experienced—even better than when our North Stars team went to the Stanley Cup finals. This season really was better.

"Our first two years with the Sharks were so bad, but that wasn't unexpected with an expansion team. But it was like everyone accepted losing for two years and then, all

> "The Sharks have had a greater impact on San Jose than anything except Silicon Valley. And you could probably get an argument about that on game nights."
>
> —*Tom McEnery*

of sudden, we wouldn't accept anything but winning. There's no feeling like that. We might never see anything like it again."

There's no question that San Jose and its surrounding communities just simply went bonkers. Thousands came to watch televised road games at The Tank during the playoffs—and screamed and shouted encouragement as though their heroes off in Michigan or Ontario could hear every word.

And San Jose's team could really, really play.

The Sharks had risen from laughable losers to respectability and then considerably beyond by playing Constantine's now-famous defensive system of conservative hockey. The idea was to let the Figure-Skating Five—Larionov, Makarov, Garpenlov, Ozolinsh and Norton—free-wheel it for scoring chances whenever they could while

The Red Wings mounted a major assault throught their seven-game series, but Sharks like Arturs Irbe, Jayson More (4) and Shawn Cronin (44) defended the fort.

everyone else played cloying, tight-checking hockey designed to keep things close and let Irbe's often-miraculous goaltending decide the dicey games.

Well, that style did the job and left opponents muttering. Some self-styled hockey purists, too. Once the Sharks became truly menacing, fans and media around the league began to carp that Constantine's team was boring, that the Sharks had become successful practitioners of ugly hockey.

Those naysayers should have visited The Tank, where the thrill quotient was never in question.

As columnist Scott Ostler wrote in the *San Francisco Chronicle:* "Imagine if they happened to have an exciting team. The entire Bay Area would have to be sprayed with Valium from crop-duster airplanes."

Who cared what odd ideas they were hatching in some of hockey's crusty old cities? Excitement was never a problem in San Jose.

Or Riga. Or Moscow, for that matter.

10

unlikely hero to score the series-clinching goal against Detroit.

Which Baker did.

And of course, the populace simply went gaga over Irbe, the charming goalie with unbelievable reflexes, boundless stamina—he set an NHL record for minutes played—and just the perfect way of summing things up. San Jose fans jumped on Irbe's reference to his highest level of play ("Like wall...") and made it a slogan. The guy his teammates call Archie was more than just a sensational goaltender. He had a way with words in several languages, speaking Latvian to Ozolinsh, Russian to Larionov and Makarov and English to everyone else.

When the talented Red Wings had erased a 3-0 deficit, pulled into a 4-4 tie and seemed ready to deliver a haymaker to the reeling Sharks in the opener of the first playoff series, someone at Detroit's Joe Louis Arena adhered to that city's oldest hockey custom and flung an octopus onto the ice. The place was roaring.

Irbe was merely amused, and decided later that the octopus was a key as the Sharks rallied to win on Vlastimil Kroupa's late goal. "We were tired, and that (delay to clean up) gave us a chance to rest," Irbe told the assembled media. "I think it helped us when they threw seafoods at us."

Seafoods?

How could you help but love these Sharks?

"The reaction from the public just kept building," team executive vice president Matt Levine said. "People would call up the arena just to talk."

And they partied. Oh, how they partied. Fans not only filled The Tank game after game, they jammed sports bars and restaurants throughout the Bay Area to see the Sharks phenomenon for themselves. Downtown San Jose became a madhouse. Otherwise sane souls painted their faces black and teal, sported goofy hats and wore jerseys that said things like, "Playov 94." They hooted and howled, learned to do The Chomp in perfect unison to the "Jaws"

Sharks fans popped up all over and they got into it with full throat. But it was such an easy team to hug, what with that charming mixture of Russian Hall of Famers, castoffs from other organizations who found second lives, gutsy grinders like Odgers and center Jamie Baker (whom director of hockey operations Dean Lombardi once affectionately called "a dirtbag"). Then there was the rock-hard Errey, who became a major-league prophet when he predicted that Baker would be the

theme and gathered on street corners just to enjoy the fun of this wondrous sports miracle that had landed in their midst.

But how did it all happen?

What incredible set of circumstances possibly could have taken place that would thrust the Sharks and San Jose into the international athletic mainstream so quickly?

It seemed like one day this was an utterly toothless team with nothing more going for it than attractive uniforms, a spiffy logo and some sharp folks in the marketing department. And then the next morning,

the populace woke up to find a glorious arena downtown that hosted Pavarotti and Streisand—not to mention the new full-time tenants with sticks and helmets, those guys who suddenly leaped into Stanley Cup contention and ignited full-blown hockey fever in an area previously known primarily for prunes and computer chips.

The best explanation is that a whole lot of great things occurred, one right after the other, almost in cosmic sequence.

No, the Sharks weren't very good during their first two seasons—and that's putting

Fans at Detroit's Joe Louis Arena held to a long-standing tradition by flinging an octopus on the ice during Game One, but the delay allowed the Sharks to regroup and skate off with a 5-4 victory.

it gently. They won a reasonable 17 games in 1991-92, then slumped to 11 victories and just 24 points the following year, a true disaster. "We weren't given a very good opportunity at the expansion talent to make us competitive right away," Gund said. "The most recent expansion teams (Florida and Anaheim) got to choose from a better talent pool."

If anyone wonders about the ability level of the early Sharks, consider that when San Jose opened the playoffs in 1994, not a single player who was in uniform on opening night 1991 remained on the team. Defenseman More and winger Pat Falloon were holdovers from that first team, but both were injured and inactive when Coach George Kingston's club began the 1991-92 season.

The best the Sharks could offer in their infancy were a couple of respected veterans, Doug Wilson and Kelly Kisio, who each gave the club a couple of solid seasons under horrible circumstances. But Wilson retired after the '93 season—remaining one of the Sharks organization's biggest fans—and Kisio jumped to Calgary through free agency.

As for civic craziness over hockey in San Jose, well, there wasn't any hockey in San Jose until 1993. The new arena had gone through several design changes, so the Sharks were forced into neighborhood exile for two seasons. They played in the 50-year-old Cow Palace in Daly City — forcing most fans to make a 100-mile round-trip drive for a look at the team that someday would move south.

It's true that the Sharks' image caught on immediately. The snazzy uniforms and that catchy logo were popular from the beginning, and if the Sharks couldn't win on the ice, the organization proved it could sell, sell, sell off it. Sharks merchandise was the hottest NHL item in the franchise's first year.

As the 1993-94 season approached, however, Sharks executives realized that it was time for a quantum leap. And they had no guarantee it would happen as they hoped.

"I won't kid anybody," Lombardi said. "We knew we might not have much of a honeymoon period once we moved to San Jose. We had to put a better team into the new arena. We played terrible hockey the second year at the Cow Palace, and our act had worn pretty thin by the end of the '93 season. You can only do so many light shows."

First off, Gund and Sharks president/CEO Art Savage dismissed the likeable but laid-back Kingston. Then they, along with Lombardi and player personnel director Chuck Grillo, stuck their necks out and replaced him with the hard-driving, discipline-oriented Constantine, who had worked wonders with the Sharks' International Hockey League affiliate in Kansas City. That move seems like a no-brainer now, but Constantine had absolutely no NHL experience in any capacity whatsoever.

The next thing was somehow constructing a team almost overnight—without mortgaging the future. The Sharks' long-term plan always had been to build through the draft, but only a handful of

the organization's own young players were ready for prime time during the 1993-94 season. Irbe, Ozolinsh, Falloon, maybe Ray Whitney. Everyone else was a question mark, so the Sharks reinvented themselves.

The most brilliant stroke was reuniting Larionov (who belonged to Vancouver but was playing in Europe) with his longtime linemate Makarov, who had been shipped unceremoniously from Calgary to Hartford. The Sharks got the two Russian superstars for what amounted to nothing, hoping that putting the pair back together might revive both of them.

It worked.

"I think it's arguable that Larionov and Makarov essentially saved our franchise," Lombardi said. "That's the impact they had. Things might have worked out all right without them, but I'm glad we never had to find out. Years from now, we'll all look back at what those two guys contributed and what they've meant to hockey in San Jose and around the world, and we'll feel honored that they played here."

It didn't stop with two-thirds of the old Soviet KLM line, either. The Sharks picked up Norton, Errey, Baker and Gaetan Duchesne prior to the season from teams that had little interest in keeping them. Elik was claimed on waivers from Edmonton in October and then in March, when San Jose needed one more scorer for a playoff push, Lombardi and Co. acquired winger Dahlen in a trade with Dallas.

By selling his system relentlessly—and allowing the Russians' No. 1 line to deviate from it completely—Constantine turned this disparate bunch into a good hockey team. And then into a very good hockey team.

"Everybody talks about Kevin's system, how he put in this defensive-minded system and turned things around," Los Angeles Kings coach Barry Melrose said. "But the biggest thing Kevin Constantine did was convince all those guys that they were winners. Taking a group of players who haven't

It took all sorts of heroics to hold off the Red Wings, with Arturs Irbe the last line of defense.

"Our fans are so loud it's just unbelievable. There isn't a building in the league with more noise than this. They just lift us up whenever we need it."

—*Jayson More*

More than 10,000 fans showed up despite ugly weather to salute the Sharks at the post-season rally at Guadalupe Park.

SHARKS RALLY 1994

Goalie Arturs Irbe told the appreciative crowd at the Sharks' end-of-season rally that the team's fans deserved success every bit as much as the team.

No one can say the Sharks didn't battle, even when things got tough toward the end of the playoffs. Winger Jeff Odgers (36) tried to force the action around the net by mixing it up with Toronto goalie Felix Potvin.

> **"...this story is an entire community accomplishing something that we'd all dreamed about."**
> **–Kevin Constantine**

won as a group and making them believe they should win—and then go out and do it—that's really an accomplishment."

However it was done, the mania swept in.

These new players with a new coach in a new arena opened up, yes, a new era in San Jose. By the time their magnificent season had run its course, the Sharks and their hometown had become regular fixtures on ESPN and household names everywhere people care about hockey.

"I have to admit," Odgers said after the season, "that when I first found out I was coming to play hockey in San Jose, I had to look at the map to see where I was going. But I don't think there is a hockey player or hockey fan in the world who doesn't know where San Jose, California is and how great the fans are."

After the Sharks had lost that heartbreaking

seventh game to Toronto, they came home to a tumultuous greeting. Around 10,000 people turned up on a rainy day to say thanks during an appreciation rally at Guadalupe River Park. It turned into a lovefest, with all those warm and fuzzy feelings flowing in both directions—fans to players and vice versa.

These, after all, were the folks who had stood and given the Sharks a prolonged, thunderous ovation during the final minutes of a playoff game they were losing 8-3 to Toronto—just to let the guys know everyone still cared.

"This story, this season was not about a player scoring a goal," Constantine told the crowd at the park. "It was not about a line combination getting some points. What is really neat about this story is an entire community accomplishing something that we'd all dreamed about. And I think that's what made this so special—we were able to share this all with you."

It was a magical year.

"Hopefully we'll go on and sometime soon, we'll bring the Stanley Cup here," George Gund said. "That will be wonderful. But I really don't think we'll ever experience anything quite like our first season in San Jose."

Hardly anyone ever has.

The Sharks scored their first-round upset of the Red Wings in part by taking advantage of Detroit's shaky goaltending. San Jose defenseman Jeff Norton (8) kept Chris Osgood occupied.

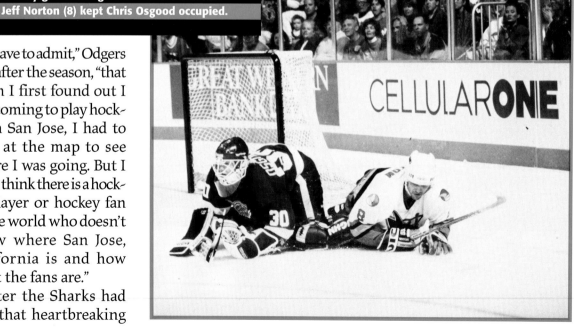

When the breakthrough season was over, Sharks coach Kevin Constantine had gone from being a virtual unknown to the target of authograph seekers.

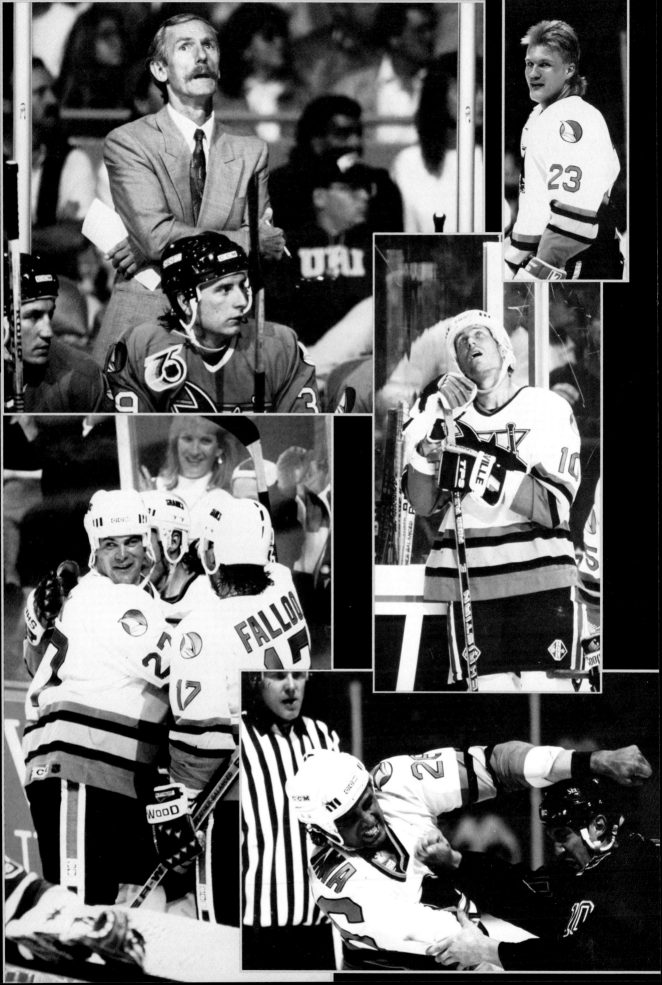

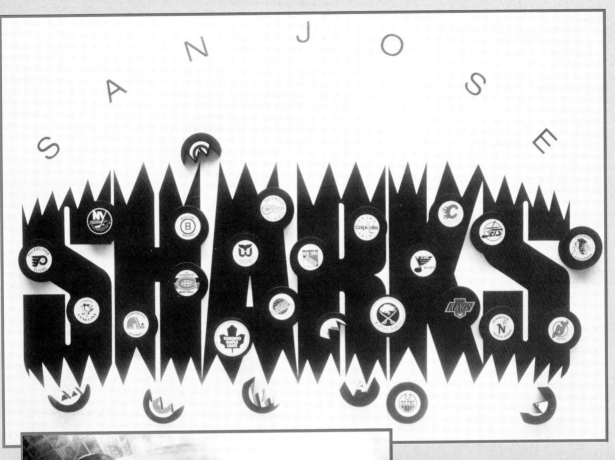

San Jose joined the major leagues for the first time when George Gund (above) announced that the Sharks would be making their permanent home in the South Bay city, then club president Art Savage (opposite page) and San Jose mayor Tom McEnery displayed the team's distinctive logo type.

Do You Know the Way to...?

You see the glimmering new arena jammed night after night. You see all that teal paraphernalia selling wildly around the globe. You see a future guided by whip-smart people in hot pursuit of a Stanley Cup.

So perhaps you see it all and believe the San Jose Sharks were born with silver hockey sticks in their mouths.

But that ain't so.

In fact, the Sharks' raging success in the Santa Clara Valley not only wasn't exactly guaranteed from the beginning, it was very much in question.

Everything's coming up roses now, but the whole thing could have come apart at dozens of junctures.

There were some strange forks in the road, to say the least.

From the time George and Gordon Gund decided in the late 1980s that they couldn't keep their NHL operation viable much longer in Minnesota until everything fell into place at San Jose

Arena during the 1993-94 season, the whole magical ride could have been derailed—at so many different points, truth be told, that Sharks executives sometimes shiver just thinking of all the nightmares they sidestepped.

"Certainly a lot of good decisions were made and calculated risks were taken that worked out well," said Art Savage, the Sharks president, "but some of the things that happened involved simple good fortune. We probably needed some luck along the way, and we got it."

What if San Jose voters hadn't approved the downtown arena after a controversial, contentious election campaign in 1988? That one was so close that then-mayor Tom McEnery once despaired that the battle might be lost.

What if a man named Howard Baldwin hadn't been badgering the NHL on behalf of a San Jose grass-roots hockey group, thus softening up the turf for

Brothers George (left) and Gordon Gund made hockey history when they announced that they were bringing an NHL team back to the Bay Area.

George Gund was willing to give up his Minnesota North Stars gear for getting a crack at seeing hockey succeed in San Jose.

Expansion to the Bay Area became official when Sharks president Art Savage (left) and owner George Gund presented the NHL with a check for $50 million.

the Gunds, who originally were thinking about an arena in San Francisco or Oakland?

What if Baldwin and the Gunds hadn't been able to reach a compromise—Baldwin called it a "global solution"—that allowed the brothers to bring hockey back to the Bay Area while giving Baldwin a chunk of their team in Minnesota?

What if fans had refused to drive from the Santa Clara Valley to watch an expansion team at the aging Cow Palace in Daly City?

What if the Oakland Coliseum's governing board hadn't been so preoccupied with the silly notion of luring Al Davis' Raiders back from Los Angeles that they virtually ignored the area's new hockey team?

What if Gund, Savage and their marketing wizard, Matt Levine, had chosen Armadillos as a nickname and decided teal was ugly?

What if everyone in the Santa Clara Valley suddenly remembered that their winter weather was just too nice to be spending time indoors and that hardly any of them knew a blue line from a phone line, anyway?

What if...?

When you look now at the way San Jose has turned into a civic dreamland for hockey, perhaps the oddest of all the major turning points concerned the Gunds' choice of Bay Area sites once they'd decided to shift their hockey operations from Minnesota to California.

Everyone agrees that the marriage with San Jose has turned out spectacularly for both sides—city and Sharks—but George Gund and Art Savage freely admit they had their eyes further north when the westward move originally was planned.

Gund had been a minority owner of the ill-

No, the Sharks weren't red-faced because it was tough to earn wins their first two seasons. But Johan Garpenlov did display a nasty sunburn following the club's first-ever road trip to Florida.

> **"Certainly a lot of good decisions were made and calculated risks were taken that worked out well, but some of the things that happened involved simple good fortune. We probably needed some luck along the way, and we got it."**
>
> *—Art Savage*

said. "Because they had an arena, and we needed one. We couldn't play out in a parking lot. I wish I could say it was a brilliant decision and we knew how everything would work out in San Jose, but that just isn't how it happened. We negotiated seriously in Oakland, with the Coliseum and the Warriors, but they weren't particularly interested in giving us a short-term lease. We didn't want a longer lease because our goal was to move into a bigger new arena somewhere.

"The irony of our talks with the Coliseum was that they accused us of just using them, trying to get a two-year lease so we'd have a place to play until the arena was ready in San Jose. But at that time, we'd never even talked to anyone in San Jose—we couldn't, because Howard Baldwin had an exclusive agreement with San Jose. Oakland never knew that."

By the way, a final light touch to this three-way arena tug-of-war came from San Francisco Mayor Frank Jordan in 1994—long after the Sharks were filling up The Tank and heading for the NHL playoffs.

"Frank wants me to move the team up to San Francisco now," Gund said, chuckling. "He says he can get an arena. I told him, 'Sorry, it's too late. Besides, San Jose is larger than San Francisco.' "

Ouch.

"You know, this has worked out better than it would have anywhere else," Gund said. "San Jose was sitting there, the 11th-largest market in the country, without a major-league sports franchise. The time was right. The arena is beautiful. It turned out to be the best for everybody that we're the San Jose Sharks."

There are really two major stories that tell the tale of how the Gunds—distressed over

fated California Golden Seals back in 1975. The Seals played at the Oakland Coliseum Arena, not that it mattered at the time. The team had been so badly mismanaged before Gund and majority owner Mel Swig got involved that the franchise was doomed no matter where the games were held.

Still, when the opportunity came for hockey's return to the Bay Area, Gund was aiming for San Francisco, where he has his home. "I admit I was thinking San Francisco, not San Jose," Gund said. "There are 700,000 cars a day coming into San Francisco."

Savage laughed when recalling how everyone's gaze wound up shifting southward.

"How did we wind up in San Jose?" he

The Sharks settled on a minor league working agreement, announcing that Kansas City of the International Hockey League would be their top affiliate. Sharks general manager Jack Ferreira (left) held up a Kansas City Blades sweater, while Blades owner Russ Parker returned the favor.

the failing fortunes of their Minnesota North Stars—wound up with a delightful new team in San Jose's spectacular arena. The first concerns the Gunds themselves, and the complicated, protracted negotiations they battled through just to ensure hockey's return to the Bay Area. The other half of the equation spotlights San Jose Arena—how it was proposed originally, the brutal election battle required to approve it and then all the 11th-hour revisions the city and Sharks undertook to make the

downtown palace a suitable venue for the NHL.

First, the Gunds.

"George has been involved in hockey practically all his life," Savage said. "He started the college hockey program at Case Western, and then he had a minority ownership role with the Seals in the 1970s. That franchise moved to Cleveland, and eventually merged with the North Stars.

"I'd been living in the Bay Area since 1976 and had been George's financial advisor since '79. I remember so well a board meeting in December of 1989, with the Gunds and their advisors. The North Stars were losing money, attendance was down

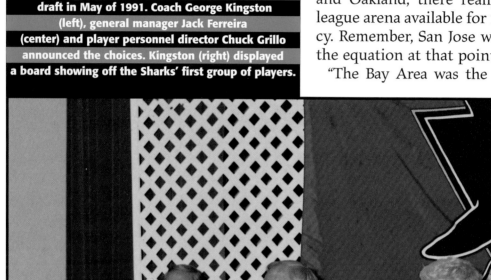

The Sharks began acquiring players at a dispersal draft in May of 1991. Coach George Kingston (left), general manager Jack Ferreira (center) and player personnel director Chuck Grillo announced the choices. Kingston (right) displayed a board showing off the Sharks' first group of players.

and we needed some cooperation from the Metropolitan Sports Facilities Commission (in Minnesota) in terms of ticket guarantees, money to put into suites (at the Met Center in Bloomington).

"The situation was pretty obvious to all of us. Expansion was coming to the NHL. You could see where new franchises would be selling for $50 or $60 million, and there we'd be, stuck in Minnesota. We needed to explore the possibility of moving the franchise."

That all makes sense in retrospect, but

why did the Gunds and Savage feel so confident about attempting a move to California, especially after the fiasco that had swallowed up the Golden Seals?

The NHL had failed once in the Bay Area and if you considered only San Francisco and Oakland, there really wasn't a major league arena available for immediate tenancy. Remember, San Jose wasn't even part of the equation at that point.

"The Bay Area was the largest market in the United States without an NHL team," George Gund said, "and things had changed quite a bit since the Seals left. It was a different situation. The Kings had made an impact in Los Angeles, so you could see that hockey could be successful in California. And we felt confident that a new arena would be built in San Francisco or Oakland."

Savage, who eventually drew the assignment of trying to make the move work, had similar feelings.

"We weren't absolutely convinced (about the Bay Area as a hockey market), but we had pretty good suspicions," he said. "There were plenty of other sports succeeding in the area—the Giants, the 49ers, the A's, the Warriors. We felt there was room for NHL hockey.

"We knew the market was changed since '75, when the Seals thing had ended, and we believed the market could be tapped. We brought Matt (Levine) in to do the research and give us the information on how to make it work."

lished Minnesota franchise to move, despite all its problems.

From January through May of 1990, the entire situation was at a stalemate. The Gunds had requested permission to move the North Stars to California, and the league resisted. At the same time, Baldwin—former owner of the Hartford Whalers—was continuing his campaign to land an expansion team for San Jose, a crusade that seemed at first blush to be

Levine, the Sharks' executive vice president who had his own sports consulting company at the time, had done projects of all sorts and at various levels for several sports franchises. He promptly launched an exhaustive market research campaign to find out everything the Gunds and Savage might have to do if hockey were to get off the ground on its second try in the Bay Area.

While all that was going on, however, the Gunds ran into a stone wall with the NHL. The league didn't want to allow the estab-

completely at cross purposes with what the Gunds had in mind.

"That was such a frustrating time," Savage said. "It felt like there was an obstacle at every turn. The league certainly presented an obstacle, just trying to move the team.

"It's strange how it all worked out. When a deal eventually was reached that satisfied everybody, there were quite a few things in it that we were unhappy with, and yet all those things turned out to be beneficial to us."

The compromise itself called for the Gunds

The Sharks' No. 1 pick in their initial entry draft in 1991 was winger Pat Falloon of Western Hockey League champion Spokane. San Jose also drafted Falloon's Spokane teammate Ray Whitney. Falloon is flanked by Jack Ferreira (left) and Chuck Grillo.

to sell the North Stars to Baldwin and Morris Belzberg—thus ostensibly keeping the team in Minnesota—in return for league approval for an expansion franchise in the Bay Area, though the new team wouldn't begin play until the 1991-92 season. That historic agreement was announced on May 9, 1990.

"It's amazing to look back at it," Savage said. "We didn't want to be out of hockey for a year, but it worked out so that was a good thing. We didn't want to wind up at the Cow Palace, but that turned out to be a perfect place for a couple of years because of the limited seating. Demand was high. It was a great place for an expansion team to play two seasons.

"And then there's the other side of it. Howard (Baldwin) didn't have the North Stars more than a couple of months. He sold out to Norman Green, (who had joined Baldwin's group at the last minute) and

Green eventually wound up getting the league's approval to move to Dallas for the 1993-94 season. And Howard wound up owning the Penguins, and won the Stanley Cup. Then we end up in San Jose, with a great arena and tremendous support. The whole thing is pretty remarkable, but when it was going on, I can guarantee you there was a lot of stress.

"There have been times along the way here when it felt like we were all in the middle of a firestorm, and nobody really knew if we'd survive it. I remember when I told my wife that my job was to come out here and make this whole thing work, and she said, 'You're nuts!'

"There were a lot of times when we all felt that way. We had to jump through an awful lot of hoops. People see the Sharks having some success now, and we've got this beautiful building, and we get into the playoffs so hockey starts catching on all over the place. Everyone assumes it was all so easy. I wish they knew how many days and nights we sweated things out, from getting the

With the completion of San Jose Arena two years away, the Sharks spent a couple of seasons in the venerable Cow Palace in the San Francisco suburb of Daly City. The Cow Palace was the smallest arena in the NHL, but that wasn't all bad: Even with a rink 50 miles from San Jose, the Sharks sold out all their home games.

Opening Night 1991: There was electricity in the Cow Palace as the NHL officially came back to the Bay Area. The Sharks also wowed their first regular-season crowd with a spectacular, unprecedented laser show.

> "There have been times along the way here when it's felt like we were all in the middle of a firestorm, and nobody really knew if we'd survive it. I remember when I told my wife that my job was to come out here and make this whole thing work, and she said, 'You're nuts!'"
>
> *—Art Savage*

franchise to getting in the arena, all of it.

"I think the first time I ever really relaxed and felt like I could take a deep breath was when the arena was opened in San Jose and I actually enjoyed a Kenny G concert."

Another facet of the Gunds' move that casual observers might take for granted is how much money was at serious risk. With San Jose Arena now up and running at capacity and the Sharks having made international news with their 1994 playoff run, the organization is turning a profit—but it's not out of the red. The Gunds paid $50 million for the expansion franchise and sunk another $34 million into arena improvements such as offices and luxury suites, then lost money during its two years at the Cow Palace, so there's a lot of work to do before those debts are paid off.

Speaking of San Jose Arena, that's another story altogether. Also another close call.

"You can't find anybody now who says they voted against the arena in 1988," former San Jose mayor Tom McEnery said. "In 1994, you'd think it passed with 100 percent of the vote."

Hardly.

The actual tally back in June of '88 was 73,409 yeas over 64,140 nays. And even that victory seemed remarkable, because pro-arena forces appeared to have run out of momentum weeks before the election and angry voices claiming that neighborhoods abutting downtown would be ruined forever were drowning out all sensible debate.

"I'm not going to kid anybody," McEnery said. "There was a time that I thought it was dead. And my political career was dead right along with the arena. Some of my friends made some gloomy jokes about that, except that it was kind of hard to laugh."

But to back up from the election just a bit: It's fairly fascinating how the down-

Sharks owners George Gund (white tux) and Gordon Gund (second from right) welcomed the crowd during ceremonies commemorating the team's first-ever home game.

town arena measure even got to the voters.

Mark Purdy, former sports editor of the *Mercury News* in San Jose, wrote a column when the arena finally opened in September of 1993. Purdy went back and traced the remarkable right-off-the-streets effort that brought the arena to a public vote and ultimately, to reality.

Let Purdy retell the story:

"Do you know how this started? It was 1984. Nine long years ago. A guy named John Neece invited me to lunch. 'We need an arena in this city,' Neece said with more intensity than I've ever seen a man show over chicken soup.

"...His idea was for a 16,000-seat building somewhere along Monterey Road on the fairgrounds property. Problem was, Neece had no financing available to pull off the arena project. The idea languished.

"That's where Chris Panopulos entered the picture. An avuncular retired accoun-tant with a gravelly voice, he formed a grass-roots organization called Fund Arena Now (FAN). The group of 30-odd people held meetings anywhere it could find, including at least one downtown tavern. There were letter-writing campaigns to the city council. There were media releases.

" 'We're going to keep it up until a San Jose arena is built,' Panopulos would growl happily at the end of every meeting. I must admit, I thought he was slightly crazy. Tuesday, when the curtain dropped and exposed the shiny A-R-E-N-A letters out-side the front entrance, I was thinking of him and the other FAN members.

"I was thinking about Joe Frizzi in partic-ular. He was a driver for a local computer company. And he was on a mission to get San Jose a major league team. This was back in 1987 or so, three years before the National Hockey League even announced it wanted to expand.

The Sharks scored a dramatic overtime victory over Calgary to kick off their maiden season at the Cow Palace. The entire bench overflowed onto the ice following Kelly Kisio's game-winning goal.

Coach George Kingston was a patient teacher who tried to steer the young Sharks through tough waters in their first two seasons.

Even with the expansion Sharks struggling, the home crowds stayed loyal. Fans also got to see plenty of visiting NHL stars, however, like Pittsburgh's Mario Lemieux.

"At his own expense, Frizzi printed up a brochure that touted San Jose's assets and potential. He sent it, also at his own expense, to National Hockey League owners. Frizzi then sent regular updates on the arena situation—even when there was no arena situation to report.

"The results were quite amazing. For months afterward, whenever an NHL owner was quoted about possible expansion, he would usually include a phrase like, '...and we also have to consider San Jose.' This, even though no city officials were yet pursuing a franchise.

"But soon, that changed. McEnery met with Neece and literally took his idea downtown, where it absolutely needed to be. McEnery's council, responding in part to the FAN people, got off the dime. Frizzi's brochure laid the groundwork for a downtown lawyer named Jim Hager to lead the pursuit of an NHL franchise that became the Sharks.

"In print, it looks so simple. It wasn't. Convincing 73,409 people to agree on anything in America today is a minor miracle. But it happened."

Purdy's phrase—a minor miracle—certainly seemed appropriate to McEnery and his supporters as election day approached in 1988. Arena proponents were besieged by residents who lived relatively close to the building site on West Santa Clara Street, people who had been frightened by talk of falling property values, traffic hassles and so forth.

"Then toward the end, opponents just kept coming back to the question of cost, raising that issue over and over," McEnery said. "We had started the campaign on the high road, proposing an arena that would be the cornerstone of San Jose's future—without spending general fund tax dollars—and that seemed solid enough. But the closer we got to election day, the more the voters in the middle seemed to be hearing all that shouting about cost, cost, cost. In this day and age, it's not hard to cast doubt on almost anything by

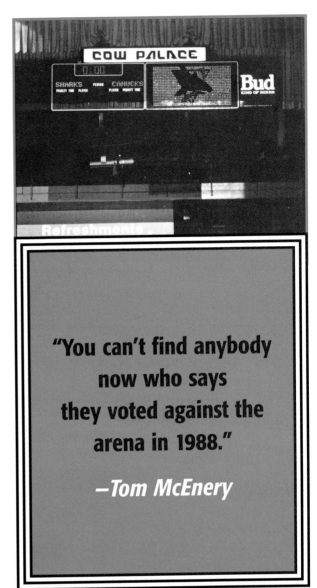

"You can't find anybody now who says they voted against the arena in 1988."

—Tom McEnery

hollering long and loud about cost.

"We had to change our strategy drastically to turn things around, and we did. We went against all conventional wisdom by releasing our polls that showed we were losing. At press conferences and other gatherings, we talked about what a defeat would mean for the San Jose of the future. It would be a failure to look past the short term. We went out after people with gusto."

McEnery cut a TV commercial with former Olympic figure skater Peggy Fleming, in which they talked about the proposed building. Fleming concluded by saying, "I'll never skate in this arena." McEnery then added: "And I won't cut the ribbon.

> "Do you know how this (arena) started? It was 1984. Nine long years ago. A guy named John Neece invited me to lunch. 'We need an arena in this city,' Neece said with more intensity than I've ever seen a man show over chicken soup."
>
> *—Mark Purdy*

But this is so important to the people of our community."

That last-minute blitz carried the day. The arena was approved.

And so, you'd think, the two story lines happily converged. George Gund brought his hockey team to northern California, discovered the only acceptable new arena was this magnificent colossus in San Jose and a wonderful marriage was promptly arranged.

Not quite.

"The building that the city had planned was a community arena," Savage said. "It wouldn't have worked for big-league hockey. The only way we could go to San Jose was if the arena were redesigned. We knew it would set us back a year, but it was the only way. We had to tell the city that without the redesign, there was no deal."

Frank Jirik, Executive Vice-President of Building Operations, who had run the Met Center back in Minnesota and moved west with the Sharks organization, remembers his first look at the plans for San Jose Arena. "Right away I saw the footprint was too small," Jirik said. "I thought: With suites in this building, it'll knock the seating capacity down to 14,000. This won't work at all."

There were other problems, too, some of which seem slightly amusing now. For instance, there was no press box in the original plans.

So it was back to the drawing board. Jirik and Vice-President Tom Goddard found themselves in almost non-stop negotiations with the city, haggling back and forth about what could be done and what couldn't—and what it all would cost. But the bottom line was that the building was indeed redesigned to suit the Sharks who, after all, were going to be the primary tenants.

The hitch, of course, was that all the extra work kept the Sharks in the Cow Palace a year longer than they'd planned. During the club's second season, the front office was literally required to operate in two places at once—San Jose and Daly City. Jirik and others had to give constant attention to the construction taking place on Santa Clara Street, but hey, there were also hockey games to conduct at the Cow Palace.

"That was a crazy year," Jirik said. "We had people at the DeAnza and Fairmont (hotels) and it seemed like we were always spreading designs all over the floors. There were days when we'd be up to our ears working on the building and all of a sudden, somebody would say, 'Oh, my God, it's 3 o'clock. We've got a game at the

Celebration in San Jose: Former NHL president John Ziegler demonstrated some hockey skills for mayor Susan Hammer.

Cow Palace.'"

During the 1992-93 season, while the Sharks were setting records for on-ice futility with their horrendous 11-71-2 record, the club's sales force was turning in a performance back in San Jose that was utterly amazing. Using only a model constructed in a downtown office building as a selling tool, the Sharks sold out every one of their luxury suites in the new arena for 1993-94.

"Every single suite was sold before any of the buyers ever laid eyes on one in the arena," Levine said.

Great expectations seemed close enough to touch, but even at the last, everyone was holding his breath. Jirik remembers fretting

over construction being held up by rain—after a seven-year drought, of all things.

But at last, the great day came and San Jose Arena was opened to the public with all the usual speeches, dignitaries and so forth. Gawkers were invited to step in and roller skate on the spanking new floor. And one and all could look around and say: Yes, this place is magnificent.

Who could have imagined, with all the yelling back and forth in 1988, that this building—soon enough dubbed The Shark Tank—quickly would be considered one of the finest in all of professional sports, what with its 64 spiffy suites, outstanding sight lines, spectacular video screen, private club

Veteran defenseman Doug Wilson came from the Chicago Blackhawks to become the Sharks' captain and also their first representative at the NHL All-Star Game.

Sometimes the early years were a struggle, as young goalie Arturs Irbe showed. But the Sharks improved, and so did Irbe, eventually leading the club into the NHL playoffs in 1993-94.

lounge (accommodating 3,000) and a first-class restaurant, along with a host of other amenities?

And then, just for good measure, the Sharks moved into their classy new home and immediately made an astounding run into the Stanley Cup playoffs. After all the raw nerves, the mighty risks, the sweating out of league decisions, the ups and downs of finding an arena and making it right—after all of that, the Sharks were hugely rewarded for their odyssey.

And so was the city of San Jose.

Whenever newspaper types or TV crews from New York, Washington and other big-name cities would come flocking around in the spring of '94, someone would invariably want to invoke some supposedly quaint reference to that dusty old Dionne Warwick tune, "Do You Know the Way to San Jose?"

The locals finally could laugh it off. The Sharks were big-time, so was their arena, and now so was the city. "Nobody's singing that song anymore," Mayor Susan Hammer sniffed to one out-of-town reporter.

Like it or not outside the Santa Clara Valley, the arrival of major-league hockey and the revitalization of downtown San Jose at last had fit together to create a bona fide success story. And at least one participant believed there was a moral in it.

"What it proved," McEnery said, "is that no matter what obstacles there are, grand things are still possible at the local city level. Anyone who doesn't believe that is welcome to come and see the San Jose Sharks."

At the Sharks' last game in the Cow Palace, the team went out scrapping and then skated around the ice, tossing Frisbees to their fans.

Redesigns forced an extra year of construction on San Jose Arena, but the Sharks' glittering new home turned out to be worth the wait.

Looking at a new home: While San Jose Arena was under construction, management and fans alike could look at a model of the Sharks' new home and imagine what it would be like to have the NHL arrive at last in San Jose.

Kelly Kisio was the Sharks' leading scorer and made the All-Star team during their rugged second season, but he left for Calgary via free agency at the close of the 1992-93 season.

Sharks game tickets for their first season in San Jose were graced with artwork dipicting the city's colorful history.

**Like it or not outside
the Santa Clara Valley,
the arrival of
major league hockey
and the revitalization
of downtown San Jose
at last had fit together
to create a bona fide
success story.**

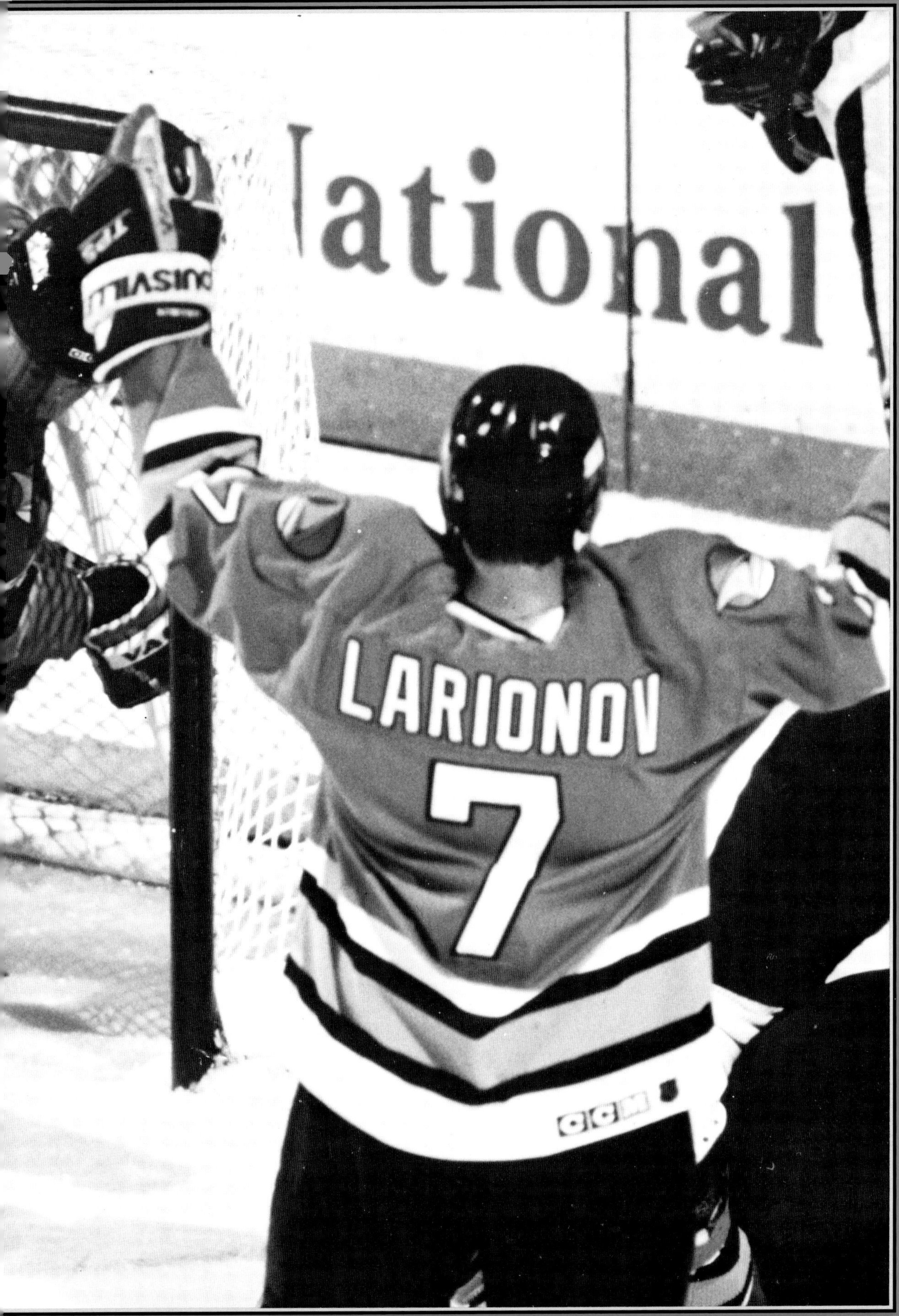

ational
LARIONOV
7
CCM

HERE'S TO THE
GREATEST SPORTS
FANS IN THE BAY AREA!

KEEP ON CHOMPIN'
AND HAVE ANOTHER
"FINTASTIC"
SEASON!

The Sharks

The Sharks made a bold decision when they gambled by naming untested Kevin Constantine (with director of hockey operations Dean Lombardi) as head coach prior to the 1993-94 season. It turned out to be one of the best moves in the franchise's brief history.

THREE

The Gospel According to Kevin

The hockey world wasn't exactly set a-tremblin' on the 16th of June 1993, when the Sharks called a press conference to reveal the identity of their new coach.

Oh, if one of the NHL's larger-than-life figures—say, Scotty Bowman—had strolled behind the podium that day and announced that he was intending to drag a lifetime of Stanley Cup know-how into the Santa Clara Valley, perhaps that might have stirred all those Molson's drinkers throughout North America.

Instead, after a marathon 58-day search, the Sharks introduced Kevin Constantine.

The new man certainly appeared earnest and tough enough, what with that drill-sergeant haircut and no-nonsense manner, but Constantine was just 34 years old—younger than Sergei Makarov, among others— and never had

played or coached a day in the NHL. In fact, until a rapid and very recent rise behind the bench at a few minor-league stops, Constantine's resume looked like something that would baffle the receptionist at an employment agency. He'd been a construction worker, bar bouncer, car salesman and part-time lift-line worker at a ski resort, just to name a few of his gainful pursuits.

San Jose's coach of the future? Was this just some guy desperate for a decent-paying job or a fellow with some legitimate chance to work miracles?

Forgive NHL lifers if they yawned at Constantine's elevation from the Sharks' International Hockey League affiliate at Kansas City to guardianship of a franchise that had bumbled to a 28-129-7 record in the first two seasons since its expansion birth.

News flash: Bad, bad team signs an unknown coach—who could get excited?

Dean Lombardi made no secret of the fact that he needed to find several impact players to reverse the Sharks' fortunes following a 71-loss disaster in 1992-93.

unusual, even by the what's-next standards of the Bay Area. Constantine confessed that he was light-years removed from the NHL's good old boy network, that he didn't scurry off to summer coaching clinics, that in fact he'd only seen a few NHL games in person.

Heroes?

The player Constantine recalled was Pete Wasalavich, who couldn't get any closer to the hockey Hall of Fame than as a ticket-buying visitor. Waslavich had been a goalie—as was Constantine—at the high school in Kevin's hometown, International Falls, Minn.

Yes, Constantine did do some name-dropping. He talked about Bill Walsh, Bobby Knight, Don Shula, Lou Holtz, Pat Riley and a few other household names. Not because he knew any of these gentlemen, mind you, but because he had spent countless hours studying their methods of success—how they taught, motivated, inspired. At one point, Constantine referred to a passage in Riley's autobiography in which the basketball coach discussed how he challenged Kareem Abdul-Jabbar, an outright Hall of Famer and unstoppable scoring machine, to become a better defensive player.

How the great ones do it clearly had been occupying Constantine's thoughts for a long time, and he didn't mind admitting it.

There was no doubting Constantine's commitment, however, nor his don't-bother-me-with-guff demeanor. Even potential skeptics conceded from the instant they laid eyes on the guy that Kevin looked the part for which the Sharks had chosen to cast him.

"The first thing that strikes you about Kevin Constantine is his face," wrote columnist Ray Ratto in the *San Francisco Examiner.* "It looks, well, mostly it looks like a fist with red hair around the knuckles.

Against the most ludicrous odds, however, Constantine began that very first day to suggest that perhaps San Jose was greeting a young man on course with destiny. If the assembled media shuffled and steadied itself for the usual string of platitudes about patience, about looking down the road at long-term building programs and so forth, it was in for a surprise.

"You can sit around all day watching MTV and dreaming about being a musician," Constantine said, his bright eyes burning holes in all those rolling cameras, "or you can pick up a guitar and try to play it."

Clearly, Kevin had chosen to play. And by God, his players soon enough would be making the same choice—or they wouldn't be his players long enough to send out a load of wash.

That entire first press conference was

It's hard to turn over more than half a hockey team's roster in a single year, but the Sharks did it with stunning effect in 1993-94. Prior to the season, they acquired solid veterans Bob Errey (top right), Jeff Norton (background) and Gaetan Duschesne (lower right).

The biggest breakthrough in personnel was the acquisition of Igor Larionov (7) and Sergei Makarov (24), who had played for years together with the great Soviet teams of the 1980s. Side by side, Larionov and Makarov anchored a free-wheeling No. 1 line that pushed the Sharks into the playoffs.

Young defenseman Sandis Ozolinsh (6) and left wing Johan Garpenlov (10) joined Jeff Norton and the two Russian stars, Larionov and Makarov, to form the Sharks' top scoring group.

"His eyes are small and piercing, the textbook definition of beady. He slaps that earnest look on you, and all of a sudden you feel like the deer, and he's the headlights. He has that kind of jaw that could pull the cherry out of a grapefruit half. His hair is short and at attention, like a million little antennae pulling information out of the air. He does not look like the sort of guy you'd want to mess with in a bar when you've had a snootful and he hasn't."

Constantine has insisted all along that quite often his face belies what's going on inside, that he really might be laughing or lighthearted when all you see is granite. He's said that the job description—especially for one so young and untested—demanded that he keep up the stone face.

And Constantine has thrown in a joke or two in the year-plus he's coached the Sharks. He's no threat to David Letterman but, yeah, Kevin can be funny. Really, though, that initial impression was just about right. Kevin Constantine came aboard with a serious thing for winning, and he wasn't counting on levity or one-liners to earn his keep. Just an improving hockey team.

"I'll tell you how driven Kevin is," said Sharks Director of Player Personnel Chuck Grillo. "At our summer camp in Minnesota (which Grillo owns and where Constantine has been a staff member), his office is right next to mine. And when he wants to tell me something, he sends me an E-mail. He's that busy, planning and working and preparing. The only time he walks into my office is either when he's got a legal pad in his hand or when he's coming in to get something out of the refrigerator and

> "You can sit around all day watching MTV and dreaming about being a musician or you can pick up a guitar and try to play it."
>
> **—Kevin Constantine**

walks right back out. If he's got something to say that's short and sweet, it's E-mail. He doesn't take time to chat, even with me."

Once Constantine unleashed his iron will and disciplined system of hockey on the NHL during the 1993-94 season, steering the previously laughable Sharks into the playoffs on his first try, it became awfully easy to gaze back and see what a canny move the organization made promoting him from Kansas City—where he'd won a league championship and almost stolen another when he had no right even to be close.

But the truth is that hiring Constantine constituted a very tough call for everyone in the Sharks hierarchy, from George Gund on down.

Grillo, who is more or less the Sharks' Godfather in all hockey matters, loved Constantine from the beginning and considered him a natural. "Some guys just have it," Grillo said. "Almost from the day I saw Kevin working with players—guys at any level—I believed he belonged in the NHL and not only that, but that he could become one of the best of all time. That's saying a lot, but that's how much Kevin's ability strikes you. He's just way ahead of his age. Kevin could be successful at anything."

Still, the business of timing in the Bay Area made the choice a lot more difficult that it seems in retrospect.

"We'd finished up that 1992-93 season with a terrible team that wasn't even playing very hard at the end," Sharks Director of Hockey Operations Dean Lombardi said. "Sure, we'd had some injuries to key guys (Sandis Ozolinsh, Pat Falloon) that made

Kevin Constantine brought a lot of positives to the Sharks' coaching job, but preparation was one of his most obvious strengths. During training-camp study sessions, Constantine prepared for the uphill battle that faced his team.

things even worse than they might have been, but let's face it: We were really bad.

"It's really unfair to blame George Kingston, who is a patient guy and seemed like the perfect coach for a young team trying to feel its way the first couple of years. But the truth is that with the record we had (71 losses, most ever in NHL history) and with fans starting to stay away or leave early, we had a credibility problem going into the new arena in San Jose.

"There was pressure to go get a name guy, a coach people knew, a guy who could give us credibility before we ever played a game in 1993-94. And there were people like that available. Scotty Bowman was out there. It definitely would have been the easy route to hire someone like that to take some of the heat off."

Credit Gund, Savage, Lombardi and Grillo for resisting the temptation. Instead, they listened and believed when Constantine stormed through his interview session with a passion, preparedness and single-minded vision that made

everyone sit up straight.

There was another bonus coming around from that interview process, as well. The other young coach who impressed the Sharks brass was Wayne Thomas. Once the decision was made to hire Constantine and nobody else in the league jumped on Thomas, the Sharks offered him an assistant's job—so San Jose wound up with both Constantine and Thomas on the same staff.

It was aggressive stuff. To use Constantine's phrase, the entire Sharks organization decided to pick up the guitar instead of sitting around watching MTV.

In hindsight, there were hints from the very beginning that the Sharks had handed over the reins to someone special. One of Constantine's first decisions was to invite veteran players as well as prospects to a July mini-camp in Minnesota. A lot of them showed up, and they were impressed.

"He has a huge will to win," Falloon said of Constantine after that summer introduction. "He seems like a real dedicated man. He wants everyone to come to (train-

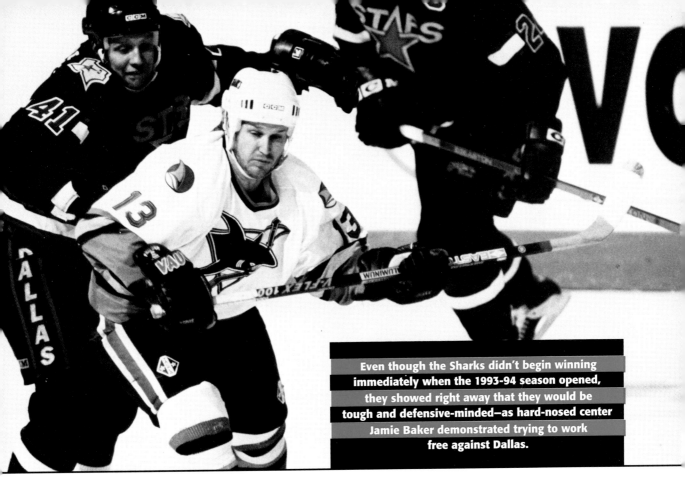

ing) camp in shape. Our first exhibition game is seven days into training camp, so we'd better be in shape."

Grillo recalled Constantine's first team gathering in Minnesota. "It could very well have been the best meeting I've seen in my 14 years of (pro) hockey," Grillo said. "There was a wave of excitement that went through the room. Everyone saw the positive direction we were going in."

One of the summer campers was veteran Russian star Igor Larionov, heading back to the NHL after a year of no-pressure hockey in Europe. "Larionov was really excited," Grillo said. "He said it reminded him of two years ago in Vancouver, when the team started to turn around."

Obviously, however, the Sharks weren't going to leap from the 11-71-2 abyss of 1992-93 to anything approaching respectability on coaching alone, no matter how hard Constantine worked. Lombardi, Grillo and their army of scouts had to find players. If the first season in San Jose Arena was going to represent any

kind of leap forward, the talent level had to be improved. Dramatically.

"One element that played into the situation was expansion," Lombardi said. "We knew that Florida and Anaheim would be getting better players than we'd had available to us a couple of years earlier. So the pressure was on us. The hockey people understood that those new teams were going to have more talent than in the earlier expansion, but we also realized that the average fan wasn't going to care about that. Fans weren't going to be too kind if Florida and Anaheim jumped right over us and had better records than we did when we were in our third year.

"That put the heat on to find talent. But on the other hand, expansion helped us, too, because it put quite a few teams in a numbers bind. They had protection problems. Some veteran players who wouldn't have been available to us were out there because teams knew they might just lose them in the expansion draft. That's how we

got (Gaetan) Duchesne and (Jeff) Norton in trades for draft choices. Same thing with Jimmy Waite, who we needed as a backup goalie for (Arturs) Irbe."

Right off the bat, the Sharks had added three legitimate NHL players. Later in the summer of '93, they snatched veteran forwards Bob Errey—who'd played on two Stanley Cup winners at Pittsburgh—and Jamie Baker off the waiver wire.

The cupboard was filling up.

But the most ingenious stroke was acquiring both Larionov and Makarov, who had played heroically side by side on the great Soviet international teams of the 1980s. Larionov had been left unprotected by Vancouver when he'd jumped to Europe and the Sharks claimed him. "It was one of the few things we did right in '92," Lombardi said. "Give George and Chuck credit for going over to Europe and convincing Igor to come back, convincing him we were going to take some big steps forward."

Grabbing Makarov was an even more spectacular move. The Sharks may long remember June 6, 1993—NHL draft day—as one of the

The season had its ups and downs early on. Rob Gaudreau got knocked airborne against Winnipeg and captain Bob Errey (on ice) was one of several Sharks who suffered injuries that kept the lineup from staying intact until midseason.

were convinced that Kozlov—their top choice—would still be available at the sixth spot in the first round. So San Jose exchanged first-round picks, and as a result acquired the Whalers' second- and third-round choices as well as future considerations.

The consideration turned out to be Makarov. Meanwhile, San Jose took Kozlov at No. 6, Kroupa with Hartford's second-round choice and a talented Finn, Ville Peltonen, with the Whalers' third-round pick. "The bottom line is that we got four hellish players and didn't give up anything," Grillo said.

Ironically, there were doubters at the time the trade was made. Quebec's Pierre Page was quoted as saying the exchange was an absolute steal—for Hartford.

Not exactly.

Makarov rammed in 30 goals in a remarkable comeback season playing alongside Larionov and helped the Sharks reach the conference semifinals. Kroupa developed rapidly during the year and became a key defenseman by playoff time. Kozlov remained in Russia through '94 but he's projected as a Sharks star of the future. And so is Peltonen, who will play in Finland during the 1994-95 season and then, hopefully, step into the lineup in San Jose. He is currently one of the captains of the Finnish National Team.

"You've got to work hard at the planning and scouting of these things, and then you've lot to be lucky, and we were," Lombardi said. "But Makarov was a godsend. That trade could turn out to be our Herschel Walker deal—like the trade where the Dallas Cowboys sent Walker to Minnesota for a whole group of players who turned them into a contender."

By the time the Sharks opened the regular season in October of 1993, only six

turning points in franchise history. San Jose owned the second overall pick in the draft and had its eye on 6-foot-5 Russian winger Viktor Kozlov. The Sharks' brain trust also liked young Czech defenseman Vlastimil Kroupa, who had gone unnoticed to the point that he wasn't even ranked by the central scouting bureau. "Kroupa was a guy that George Gund really, really liked," Grillo said.

Just before the draft, the Sharks found themselves with the opportunity for a deal with Hartford, which coveted the No. 2 pick. The key to a trade was that the Sharks

players remained from their opening-day roster the previous season. The talent pool had been upgraded spectacularly.

"I remember at training camp how the reporters covering the team kept mentioning how much more ability there was on the ice," Lombardi said. "They'd tell me that the first two years, the only guy to watch with any skills was Falloon. Now there were guys with ability all over the place. We didn't know how much better we would be, but we guessed it was a lot."

Grillo was more specific. To the sound of much laughter, he told friends around the league that the Sharks would record 76 points, which sounded pretty crazy since they'd only scraped out 24 the year before. "I admit I was wrong about the 76 points," Grillo said. "We wound up with 82. Nobody was laughing anymore."

For all of their maneuvering, however, the Sharks still couldn't avoid a horrendous start when the long-awaited first season at San Jose Arena finally got going.

Despite vastly improved talent and depth, despite Constantine's fierce will and the fact that he'd whipped these new-look Sharks into top shape, despite an emotional lift from their spectacular new home, the Sharks fell flat on the ice with an 0-8-1 start that, frighteningly, reminded doubters back home of all those sorry nights during the first two seasons. In those first nine games, the Sharks managed only a home-ice tie with Boston and only scored more than two goals once, in a 6-4 loss to Vancouver.

Irbe, for one, was horrified.

"Oh, my God," he said. "What's going on? We really don't deserve this to be happening to us again like last season. We have a better team than this."

The light at the end of the tunnel finally showed up on Oct. 26, when all sorts of good things happened. First of all, in the wee hours of the morning, Constantine got a phone call from the office. Edmonton, which happened to be in town, had placed center Todd Elik on waivers and Lombardi

All the Sharks, including promising young winger Pat Falloon (17) and center Todd Elik (27), kept looking to Constantine for direction.

Hockey fever in San Jose reached a higher pitch on Feb. 13, 1994, when the Sharks completed a three-game sweep of Chicago with a 1-0 victory at The Tank. Sandis Ozolinsh (behind Igor Larionov) scored with less than a minute to go in the dramatic duel, and the Sharks erupted when the game ended.

wanted to claim him. He was checking with Constantine, who was almost too groggy to understand the conversation.

But the claim was made, and Elik changed sides prior to game time—though Constantine barely remembered it.

"With the way things were, the coaches and I went out and really got a workout," Constantine said. "We went out on the rink and I worked up a sweat for the first time in a couple of months. By the time I got done and then went out and got a steak, I was really beat and went home and fell asleep.

"In the morning when I got up, I told Peggy, 'Honey, I think I talked about something important last night, but I'm not sure.'"

There was more good news: Larionov, who had missed the first nine games with a shoulder injury, was at last was ready for action. And it's impossible to overstate Larionov's importance to the 1993-94 Sharks. Over the course of the regular season, they were 30-20-10 when Igor was playing, 3-15-6 when he was out with injury or illness.

The Sharks even bowed to superstition on this particular night. Constantine reverted to a tradition he and his wife had practiced in Kansas City—Peg drove him to the game. And winger Jeff Odgers discovered that a lucky penny he always kept taped to the bottom of his skate has disappeared, so he replaced it with a new one.

And blessedly, the season-opening winless streak was over.

The Sharks whipped Edmonton 3-1 with Irbe outstanding in net, Larionov scoring the first goal and Elik assisting on the third. The greatest turnaround in NHL history had begun, though all Constantine could say afterward was, "This feels a whole lot better than losing."

The rest of the season, of course, gradually turned into a fairy tale. The Sharks

The Sharks demonstrated that they wouldn't be bullied, even by the league's toughest players. That's Rangers brawler Ty Domi getting a shove into the boards from Jamie Baker.

first got comfortable with Constantine's defensive-minded system ("It takes a little more selling than the idea of playing offense," he said...) and then discovered that with Irbe in net, the first line of Larionov, Makarov and Johan Garpenlov teaming with defensemen Ozolinsh and Norton zooming around to create goals with their bang-bang passing and everyone else committed to smart play and tight checking, well, they could play with anyone.

En route to their rather remarkable 33-35-16 record, the playoff upset over top-seeded Detroit and that seven-game marathon with Toronto, the Sharks came upon several important turning points. Each time, they learned something new about themselves and cranked their game up yet another notch.

First of all came Constantine's accommodation with the Russians.

The young coach had preached defense and discipline from the first day of training camp, believing that sound hockey—even if not especially pleasing to the eye—could be successful at any level, including the NHL. The problem was that Larionov and Makarov were used to freelancing in that wide-open, move-and-pass style the Soviets had made famous while changing the face of international hockey. Garpenlov was comfortable at wing with that type of play, and it suited the gifted young defenseman, Ozolinsh, as well.

There was some butting of heads. Much later, Constantine would joke about Makarov and admit, "I don't say anything to Sergei. No. 1, there's nothing that I could

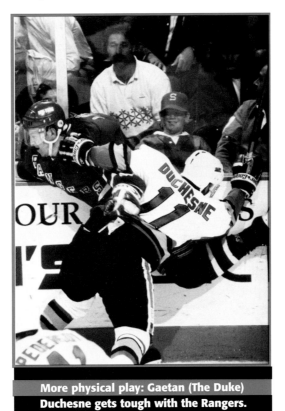

More physical play: Gaetan (The Duke) Duchesne gets tough with the Rangers.

tell him that could do any good and No. 2, he doesn't listen to anything I say, anyway."

In the beginning, though, Constantine really had planned for the whole team—Russians included—to hurl themselves into his tight-checking, shut-down-the-ice type of game. But Larionov and Makarov were frustrated and wanted to turn up the offensive heat. They even went so far as to tell Ozolinsh when to join their rushes and when to hang back. Ozolinsh more or less obeyed, which meant he technically was ignoring the coach's demands.

Constantine could have been hard-nosed about it all, and perhaps lost the chemistry his curious team was busy creating. But instead, he thought it over and tossed his own ego—not to mention part of his system—out the window.

When the question of whose rules Ozolinsh should follow was put directly to Constantine by the media, he laughed and replied, "If you were him, who would you listen to?"

The crisis was over. The Russians and their linemates were free to roam and everyone else was asked to understand and play defense first. The combination began to click famously, and Constantine had won everyone's admiration for staying tough—while showing a willingness to be flexible and realistic, too.

The Sharks rebounded fairly quickly from that disastrous start and then passed the first serious test that proved the season might be something very special. They were 4-11-3 after opening a potentially devastating seven-game mid-November road swing with a 4-0 loss at Dallas. San Jose had been brutal away from home its first two seasons, and here came games at New Jersey, the Rangers, Washington, Boston, Hartford and Buffalo. It was a chance for a serious dive back to oblivion.

Instead, the Sharks went 3-2-1 the rest of the trip, winning at New Jersey, Washington and Hartford and tying the eventual Stanley Cup champion Rangers. Even the losses—3-1 at Boston and 6-5 in Buffalo—were thrillers than could have gone the other way. Larionov and Makarov each scored three goals in the six-game span, and so did Duchesne. Ozolinsh and Garpenlov got a couple apiece. The big line was proving to be legitimate, even in hostile surroundings.

"We went into some tough buildings and won some games," Norton said. "We learned a lot from that trip. We started to realize what we had, that we could be a pretty good hockey team."

When the Sharks got back to San Jose, they'd developed a new mentality.

Respectable was no longer the goal. After they'd beaten powerful Detroit 6-4, swept a home-and-home series against Anaheim (including Irbe's first shutout of a spectacular season), tied Winnipeg and outlasted Florida 2-1, the Sharks were 11-13-5 and—for the first time ever—they were thinking playoffs.

"Unless you're dreaming about something, you don't have anything to shoot for," Constantine said. "I've never been around a professional athlete who doesn't have a goal of some sort. We've talked about our pursuit of the playoffs. Based on that, we must assume we have a chance."

There. It was out.

Having matched its entire victory total of the previous season by Dec. 5, Team Teal officially had set its sights on the postseason. And nobody was chuckling, especially not the revved-up fans who began filling up the new arena and happily referring to it as The Shark Tank. Starting with a Dec. 15 game against St. Louis, the Sharks' growing legion of loyalists sold out The Tank for 29 of their heroes' final 31 home games in 1993-94—including the last 13. Empty seats were history.

"You start every year thinking you can

make the playoffs," Odgers said, but reality set in pretty quickly the last two years. Now, everybody in the room really believes we can make it."

And yet the Sharks had to endure one more test. They suffered through a nine-game winless streak in December (0-7-2), a skid that wasn't broken until they beat Sharks' first in 12 games without Larionov. The good news was that, even after the winless streak, the Sharks remained just about dead even with Los Angeles and upstart Anaheim for the eighth and last Western Conference playoff spot.

So they remained believers, in part because Constantine never wavered, either

With the No. 1 line finally intact after some nagging injuries and with the addition of Todd Elik and Ulf Dahlen, the Sharks were a much more potent offensive team in 1993-94. On-ice celebrations became more frequent as the season wore on.

in his approach or his certainty that the ship was sailing in the right direction. "Last season when I coached at Kansas City," Constantine said, "we lost eight games in a row. Maybe that was very healthy for me. When you lose, you do start questioning if what you're doing is right, but by going through that last year, I learned to keep the faith."

Vancouver 3-2—on the road, no less—on Dec. 31. Injuries had a lot to do with the slump. Norton, Larionov and Ozolinsh all got hurt in December. To underscore a point, that victory in Vancouver was the

Sure enough, the Sharks embarked on a 4-1-3 resurgence, and one of the ties was inspiring. Irbe was, well, "like wall" during a 2-2 tie against the Kings on Jan. 11, a game

Even though Detroit was supposed to have all the punch in its first-round series with San Jose, the Sharks displayed their own bite right from the start. Vlastimil Kroupa (26) worked over Dino Ciccarelli on the boards, Jeff Norton squared off with Wings bad boy Bob Probert and the Sharks showed surprising offensive pressure, forcing the Red Wings back on top of their own goalie, Bob Essensa.

in which the Sharks got out even despite a franchise-low 10 shots on goal. At the other end, Irbe stopped 37 of 39 attempts and disaster was averted. It was Constantine's type of hockey at its nerve-testing best.

The true jump-start for the Sharks' eventual playoff dash, though, occurred in a five-day span in early February. An odd quirk of scheduling brought the Chicago Black Hawks to California for three consecutive games—one neutral-site match at Sacramento and two more at The Tank.

The Sharks swept, dramatically.

San Jose beat former teammate Jeff Hackett 4-3 in Sacramento with Errey notching the final goal, then duplicated the score exactly at home as Elik and Makarov each scored twice against the Hawks' No. 1 goalie, Ed Belfour.

And then came one of the most exciting victories in a season full of them, as Ozolinsh broke up a marvelous goaltending duel between Irbe and Belfour by whipping home a wrist shot from the slot with less than a minute remaining to hand the Sharks a 1-0 triumph.

By this time, it was apparent that the key to the playoffs would be the Sharks' ability to keep the Kings and Mighty Ducks from gaining any significant ground in head-to-head games. Against Anaheim they were perfect, winning all six meetings. It was tougher going against the talent-rich Kings, but the Sharks hung on and even survived a bit of hockey history. The teams played back-to-back games on March 19-20, and Los Angeles won at home 2-1 on Jari Kurri's goal, spoiling a fabulous effort from Irbe.

Back in San Jose, the Kings escaped with a 6-6 tie on Wayne Gretzky's rebound with 49 seconds left—The Great One's 801st goal of a legendary career. That score tied him, quite temporarily, with Gordie Howe as the NHL's all-time leading goal-scorer.

Gretzky's heroics overshadowed an event that was far more significant for the

Sharks in that tie. Ulf Dahlen, a 6-foot-2, 195-pound right winger who could bang in the corners and light a few goal lamps, had just been acquired from Dallas in exchange for defensemen Doug Zmolek and Mike Lalor—and Dahlen scored his first San Jose goal in the second period against the Kings.

Dahlen's arrival changed the Sharks' personality. Simply put, Ulf gave the offense some teeth it had been needing—he'd scored at least 35 goals each of two previous seasons. It was no coincidence that the Sharks took off on a nine-game unbeaten streak beginning with Dahlen's first appearance.

"That trade was the first time we'd ever addressed a specific need," Lombardi said.

"Before that, we'd always just wanted to add talent. But we were in a race for the playoffs, we needed size and scoring, and we were fortunate to have enough depth on defense that we could give up a couple of good hockey players that Dallas felt it needed. It turned out to be a great deal."

Dahlen's presence set off the final rush toward San Jose's first postseason party. The Sharks got over their biggest jump in late March with a road trip to Pittsburgh, Toronto, Winnipeg and St. Louis—a scary assignment since they'd never won at their first two stops and hadn't gotten a single point anywhere against the Blues.

"That was the trip where the veterans stepped up, especially Larionov," Lombardi

> "Some guys just have it. Almost from the day I saw Kevin working with players, guys at any level, I believed he belonged in the NHL and not only that, but that he could become one of the best of all time."
>
> *—Chuck Grillo*

said. "He proved what a money guy he is. There were guys running at him, yakking at him, trying everything to get Igor off his game, and nothing bothered him. He was unbelievable. It reminded me of Joe Montana, raising his game when the stakes get higher."

In Pittsburgh, Larionov assisted on a goal by Makarov as the Sharks earned a 2-2 tie. Larionov had a goal of his own during a tense 2-1 victory in Toronto, then recorded his first Sharks' hat trick in an 8-3 blowout win at Winnipeg. And finally, as the Sharks stepped out of St. Louis with a 4-3 victory to complete an unbeaten trip, Larionov scored again and assisted on goals by Makarov and Norton.

After that trip, wrapping up a playoff spot became something of a formality. In fact, the Sharks were hunting down Vancouver and Chicago for the sixth and seventh spots in the conference as the season wound down.

Oh, it was fun.

Makarov completed a hat trick of his own against Winnipeg, not only finishing up by scoring on the first penalty shot in franchise history but calling his shot. "(Trainer) Tom Woodcock goes up to Igor and asks him where he thinks Makarov will put it," Constantine said. "Mak steps up right then and winks at them. 'Five-hole,' he said. "Damn if he didn't put it right there."

Perhaps the public didn't get to enjoy the full pleasure of Makarov's comeback season,

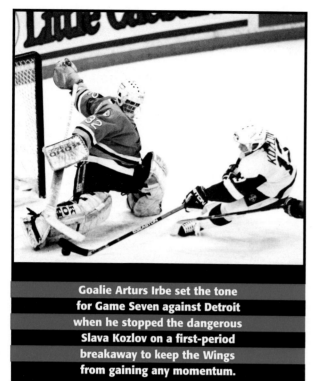

Goalie Arturs Irbe set the tone
for Game Seven against Detroit
when he stopped the dangerous
Slava Kozlov on a first-period
breakaway to keep the Wings
from gaining any momentum.

"It's something we don't need right now," Norton said of excessive satisfaction just making the playoffs. "We still have some big games left."

Still, the clincher was sweet. Kings coach Barry Melrose told the media with the straight face that the Sharks were playing the best hockey in the league right then, and Gretzky not only sent word of his congratulations to the entire Sharks team, he announced flat-out that Irbe was his choice as the NHL's most valuable player.

And in a bit of irony, George Kingston was present at the Great Western Forum to see his old team join the playoff fraternity. Given the talent—or lack of it—that Kingston scuffled with for two seasons, he must have thought the entire scene was surreal. "I'm very pleased for the players who played hard those two years," said Kingston, a very decent man who'd been in an impossible spot. "I'm pleased for them and the people of San Jose. I bled teal for two years."

Meanwhile, the league at large realized now that the Sharks were no flukes.

since Sergei is notoriously quiet and has little to say to the media. He's not surly, just content to let his actions take care of themselves. But the other Sharks could share Sergei's good times—they even nicknamed him "Freight Train" after an incident against Philadelphia in which Makarov returned to the bench after skating through and around three Flyers to score a goal, proclaiming to teammates, "Like freight train. Whoo, whoo!"

The historic playoff berth was clinched on April 5—in Los Angeles, which was fitting. The Sharks got two goals from Jamie Baker and yet another great performance by Irbe in their 2-1 victory that mathematically eliminated Anaheim.

The entire Sharks family was on hand for the big moment—Gund, Lombardi, even club president Art Savage, who interrupted a family vacation for the celebration. Typical of this team's new attitude, however, there was no champagne after the playoff-clinching, no wild locker-room histrionics. Constantine long ago had decreed that champagne is reserved for just one occasion, which is winning the Stanley Cup.

The Sharks stunned the Wings
by scoring just 47 seconds
into the seventh game.
Goalie Chris Osgood could only stare
at the offending puck as
Johan Garpenlov (10)
raised his stick in jubilation.

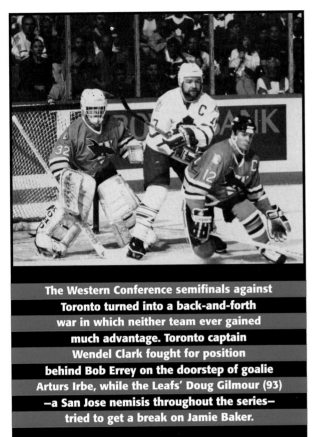

The Western Conference semifinals against Toronto turned into a back-and-forth war in which neither team ever gained much advantage. Toronto captain Wendel Clark fought for position behind Bob Errey on the doorstep of goalie Arturs Irbe, while the Leafs' Doug Gilmour (93) —a San Jose nemisis throughout the series— tried to get a break on Jamie Baker.

"You start with the backbone—goaltending," said Toronto star Doug Gilmour. "They have great goaltending. They're good offensively, and they're good defensively. They're obviously following Kevin's game plan, and following it well."

So the Sharks began setting their jaws for the playoffs, and they had no intentions of letting it be a token appearance. And frankly, their performance later against Detroit and Toronto probably shouldn't have caught North America by surprise quite the way it did. After all, the Sharks were 33-27-15 after their 0-8-1 start—a pace that would have put them at the 90-plus point level over an entire season.

"We're playing very, very well right now," Duchesne said as the regular season wound down. "I think we can be very dangerous when we get in the playoffs."

And in fact, the Sharks had been playing postseason-type hockey most of the year—tough in goal, disciplined on defense, avoiding most huge mistakes,

conservative with scoring chances. "It's almost like they're a team built for playoff hockey," said Toronto coach Pat Burns, who found out soon enough how true that would be.

Having said all that, however, the Sharks' first-round dismissal of Detroit was still something of shocker, especially the way it happened.

The teal-clad fanatics went wild, of course, when burly defenseman Shawn Cronin scored San Jose's first-ever playoff goal and Vlasty Kroupa's late rocket in Game One handed the Sharks an improbable 5-4 victory, but Detroit and its army of gunners got back on track to win the second and third games—and then the Wings took what seemed to be an insurmountable 3-1 lead in the second period of the fourth game at The Tank.

Worse, Detroit's third goal was an outright gift from Irbe, who looked as though all those NHL-record minutes played might finally be catching up to him. Irbe simply put the puck on Kris Draper's stick behind the net, then dropped his head in disgust when Draper tapped the thing into an open goal.

"A very bad mistake," Irbe said. "I

That's not debris on the ice at San Jose Arena—it's a celebration. Fans littered the rink with all sorts of headwear when Ulf Dahlen completed his three-goal hat trick during a 5-2 victory over Toronto in Game Three.

Beginning of the end: Four members of the Sharks' top unit—(from left) Jeff Norton, Sergei Makarov, Johan Garpenlov and Igor Larionov—show their disappointment after Wendel Clark's goal gave a Toronto a 2-0 lead that the Leafs would never relinquish in the seventh game of their playoff marathon.

thought: Oh, no. What a terrible time to do this. But I remember the way my teammates reacted. They told me not to worry, that they'd get the goals back, that it would be OK."

And indeed, the Sharks decided it was time to bail out the goalie who'd saved their fannies so many times all season. Larionov came right back to score and make it 3-2, then Dahlen snapped home a rebound for a 3-all tie heading into the third period.

The Tank was rocking, a perfect setting for one of the year's most gorgeous goals. Detroit was gearing up in the Sharks' zone when a puck deflected off Ozolinsh's skate to Larionov near center ice. "It was lucky," Ozolinsh said. "I was out of position."

Luck or not, beauty was coming.

Larionov zoomed down the right wing and, just at the perfect moment, as he'd done so many times in those glory days with the Soviet juggernaut, Igor slid the puck cross ice to a flying Makarov, who nudged it past sprawling goalie Chris Osgood to give the Sharks an electric 4-3 victory that had 'em dancing in the streets in downtown San Jose.

"You see some of the things those two guys do, and you're just amazed," Norton said. "The passing is just unbelievable, the sense of timing, of where they're going to be just at the perfect moment."

Makarov's explanation, as always, was succinct. "With Igor, it's like we have the same mind," he said.

The rally moved everyone. "I'm impressed and proud to be a member of this team," said Dahlen, the newest hand. "All the character we showed, all the heart we showed out there. The way guys were throwing themselves on the ice, blocking shots, breaking up plays."

The Sharks' comeback seemed to unnerve the Red Wings in general, and Osgood in particular. When Elik and Makarov scored on the Sharks' first two shots early in Game Five, Bowman yanked Osgood in favor of Bob Essensa. No matter. The Sharks won 6-4 with Garpenlov netting the clincher, and headed off to Detroit needing just one victory to complete the upset.

The angry Red Wings unleashed their full arsenal in the sixth game, however, and pummelled the Sharks 7-1. "It was embarrassing to get beaten that way," Baker said. "We know that back in San Jose, the arena is open and everybody's there rooting for us, and we came in and made every mistake you can make."

But Baker had a date with history.

Game Seven was the underdog's classic. The Sharks got early goals from Ozolinsh (just 47 seconds into the game) and Makarov to quiet the crowd and force the Red Wings into a tight, tense, possession battle that took a lot of starch out of their free-wheeling style. Irbe stoned Slava Kozlov on a first-period breakaway that might have turned the tide in the other direction. What's more, the Wings' frustration even goaded normally well-behaved superstar Sergei Federov to attack Jayson More with a savage cross-check. The favorites were coming apart.

"We put ourselves in a position to lose," grumped Red Wings defenseman Paul Coffey. "There's no use candy-coating it."

Thus the decisive game was tied 2-2 in the third period, the kind of situation the Red Wings hate and in which the Sharks had learned to thrive. And so, with 6:35 to play, Detroit made the sort of mistake that causes mighty teams to unravel.

Osgood was out of his net, trying to clear a puck by throwing it up along the boards when Baker, who had just stepped on the ice during a line change, found the thing bouncing crazily at his feet with Osgood still far out of position. Baker didn't have time to think or aim—he was too worried about getting good wood on the puck.

"I saw (Errey) right at the edge of the goal and I just wanted to get it near him," Baker said. "I wasn't really thinking the shot would go in."

But it did.

Errey, who had predicted two days earlier that Baker would score the series-clincher, did have a chance to deflect Baker's funny-looking shot. At the last second, though, Errey pulled back his stick and made himself a prophet.

After the Sharks fought off Detroit's last-gasp rushes and the greatest victory in San Jose sports history was complete, Osgood broke down in tears. The Sharks broke down in joy.

"(The Red Wings) thought we were going to give them the stupid game like we did the other night," Norton said. "You could see their frustration. On Thursday (the 7-1 victory), they were yipping and yapping and leaning over the glass. But tonight, if you looked over there, there was a bunch of starry eyes. It was perfect."

Norton added something else, too. He made it clear the Sharks wanted no part of hearing they'd somehow fallen into the second round.

"We deserved this," he said. "We never backed down. We could have been happy to be here, but we worked our asses off. We deserved to win."

Actually, the Sharks could say the same thing about the Toronto series, in which they went toe to toe, nose to nose with the favored Maple Leafs through seven emotional games—and clearly could have advanced to the conference finals if Garpenlov's Game Six overtime blast had been an inch lower and gone under the crossbar.

And yet it was still a wonderful war.

The No. 1 line's magic won the first game in Toronto, a 3-2 thriller that was decided by a play on which every Shark on the ice touched the puck before Garpenlov slid it past Felix Potvin's stick side.

Toronto squared the series at home, but Dahlen produced a dramatic hat trick as the Sharks got the gang at The Tank up and roaring with a 5-2 victory in the third game. The see-saw continued after that,

with the Leafs dominating Game Four 8-3—as Irbe sat out the last period—and the Sharks snapping back with a decisive 5-2 triumph in the fifth game. Makarov was magnificent in that one, opening the scoring on a breakaway, setting up another goal with a behind-the-back pass and later ripping home the rebound of a Larionov wrister from the slot.

Which brought the Cinderella season to Game Six, the agony of those near-misses in overtime and Gartner's funny-looking

goal to end it—a fluky thing that started when the puck took a crazy sideways bounce off Cronin's skate.

"Looking back, we outplayed them in the sixth game and had our chance to win the series right there," Norton said. "Sometimes hockey just comes down to a strange bounce. They got one, and we didn't."

Oddly, the Sharks finished the year with a fiercely contested defeat that represented a complete reversal of form. Toronto won 4-2 despite being outshot 31-21— usually a Sharks specialty—and built its lead while the red-hot Potvin was busy stopping the generally deadly Larionov twice from point-blank range.

"If we get even one of those past him, it's a different game," Larionov said, "but Potvin was very good. He was the difference."

Funny, but teams had been saying the same thing about Arturs Irbe for months. "I didn't have the performance I should have had for a Game Seven," said Irbe, as always willing to take the Sharks' fate upon his own weary shoulders. "But nobody blamed me. It was a great feeling to go this far. We just didn't get the luck in this game."

Let's leave it to the captain, Bob Errey, to put the Sharks' whole incredible run from nowhere to Stanley Cup contenders into perspective. "Not many people expected us to get this far," Errey said. "We set our goals higher than others set them for the Sharks."

It's hard to imagine anyone suggesting the Sharks didn't meet their goals in 1993-94. Just those guys in the locker room who got it into their heads that they ought to be drinking champagne from the Cup itself.

The guys who brought hockey hysteria to San Jose.

> "He (Larionov) proved what a money guy he is. There were guys running at him, yakking at him, trying everything to get Igor off his game, and nothing bothered him. He was unbelievable. It reminded me of Joe Montana, raising his game when the stakes get higher."
>
> *—Dean Lombardi*

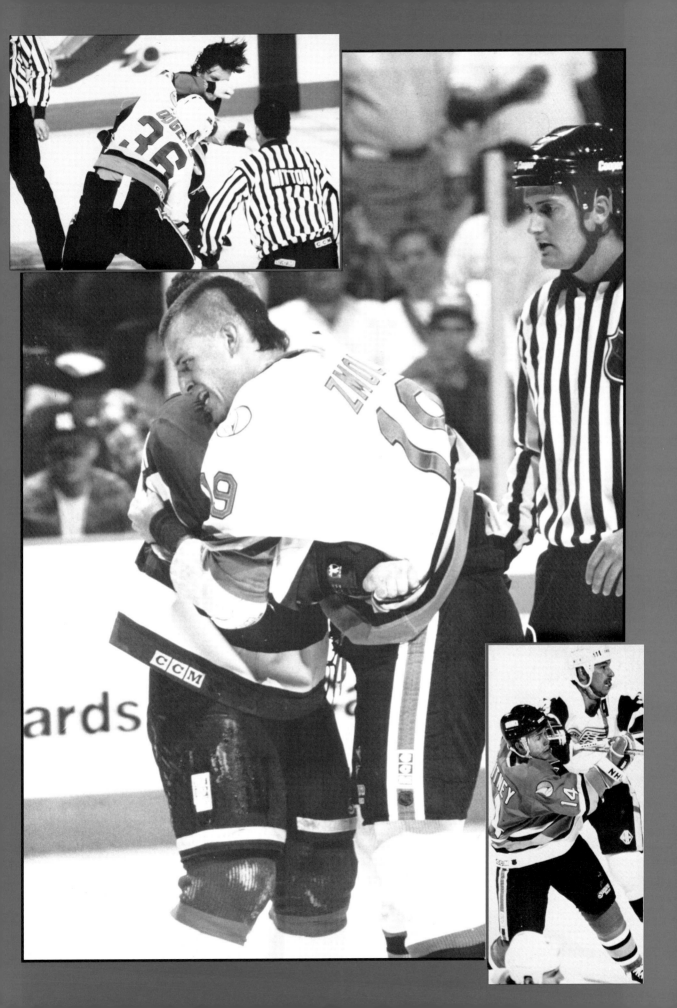

The Sharks leaped upward in the NHL standings by blending several Russian- and European-born with a group of Canadians and Americans to form the league's most diverse roster. One of the brightest stars was young Latvian goalie Arturs Irbe.

The World's Team

What makes the San Jose Sharks so unique?

Sure, they knocked the rest of the NHL quite rudely into the boards with that remarkable—and unprecedented—dash to the playoffs in their breakthrough 1993-94 season. It was heady stuff, but in the Sharks' grand scheme of things, the miracle year was simply another step.

It was all great fun, but what really separates the Sharks from their hockey brethren is the scope of their dreams. This franchise has global aspirations, and nobody's joking.

The Sharks have grander plans for world domination than Alexander the Great, and what's more, some aspects of this Santa Cruz-to-Sweden strategy already have been realized.

You surely saw that picture of Princess Diana's kid—who happens to be heir to the British throne—wearing the familiar teal-and-black ball-

Princess Diana, on ski holiday in the Austrian Alps with her sons Prince William (the Sharks fan), and Prince Harry (right) .

cap, didn't you? "At least eight people sent me that picture right away," said Sharks chief operating officer Greg Jamison.

Or perhaps you've noticed that franchise owner George Gund is considered a globe-trotting guru who's logged more miles than Henry Kissinger in a relentless pursuit of hockey talent?

Even a brief conversation with any Sharks executive leaves you with the impression that the San Jose Gang won't be satisfied until everyone on the planet owns at least one chomping-Shark sweatshirt and all the potential goalie prospects have been pulled from Siberian ore mines or some other equally obscure spot. If the Sharks need to travel on yaks or hire Sherpa guides to convert fans or seek out possible stars with unpronounceable names, well, Gund's teal-appointed private plane is fueled and ready.

Always.

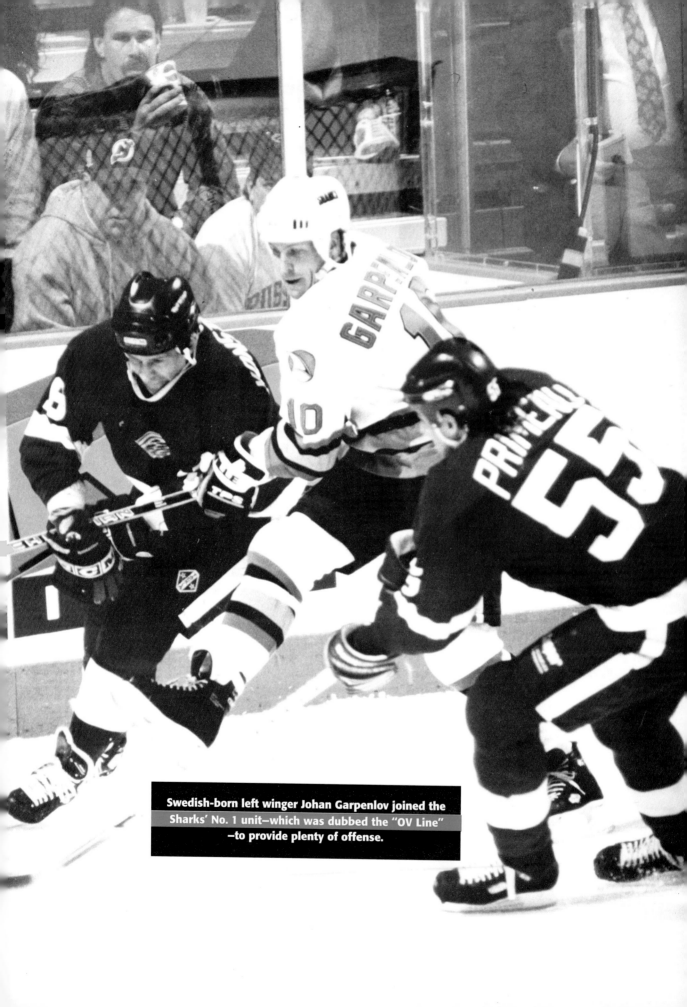

Swedish-born left winger Johan Garpenlov joined the Sharks' No. 1 unit—which was dubbed the "OV Line" —to provide plenty of offense.

"We're the guys who are always willing to pack our bags and go travel in places where it's 30 degrees below zero, looking for the players who can help," Sharks hockey operations director Dean Lombardi said.

The Sharks are hunting for fans, too—anyone who'll cheer for their hockey club and maybe even spend some hard-earned dollars—or rubles— for any item bearing that now-famous black shark. The franchise's unbelievable marketing success has reached just about everywhere—including deep into Canada, which might have been the biggest surprise of all. But visitors in Moscow spot Sharks jerseys, as well. There is a Sharks merchandise outlet in Riga, Latvia. And so on.

Latvians, in particular, have gone ga-ga over the Sharks—especially since two of the club's brightest young stars are Riga-born, goalie Arturs Irbe and defenseman Sandis Ozolinsh. When the Sharks store opened in Riga, Latvian Prime Minister Valdis Birkavs came out in person to say, "I wish all the best for our two guys and for the Sharks in the playoffs."

So imagine a drumroll in the background and prepare yourself for the Sharks' ultimate dream—the other one besides a few Stanley Cups.

"You've heard of Canada's Team, America's Team. Our goal is to become The World's Team," said Sharks player personnel chief Chuck Grillo.

Gund sees nothing but obvious logic in his Sharks' ambitions. "I think it makes sense," he said. "The world comes together with our team better than the way the rest of the world has come together. With modern communication, the world is smaller than ever. I think we have to learn to live together and to play together. It can be hard, but for us it has come together fast."

True enough.

The 1993-94 Sharks achieved the league's greatest-ever turnaround with a roster that included Americans, Canadians (both English- and French-speaking), Latvians,

> "We're the guys who are always willing to pack our bags and go travel in places where it's 30 degrees below zero, looking for the players who can help."
>
> —Dean Lombardi

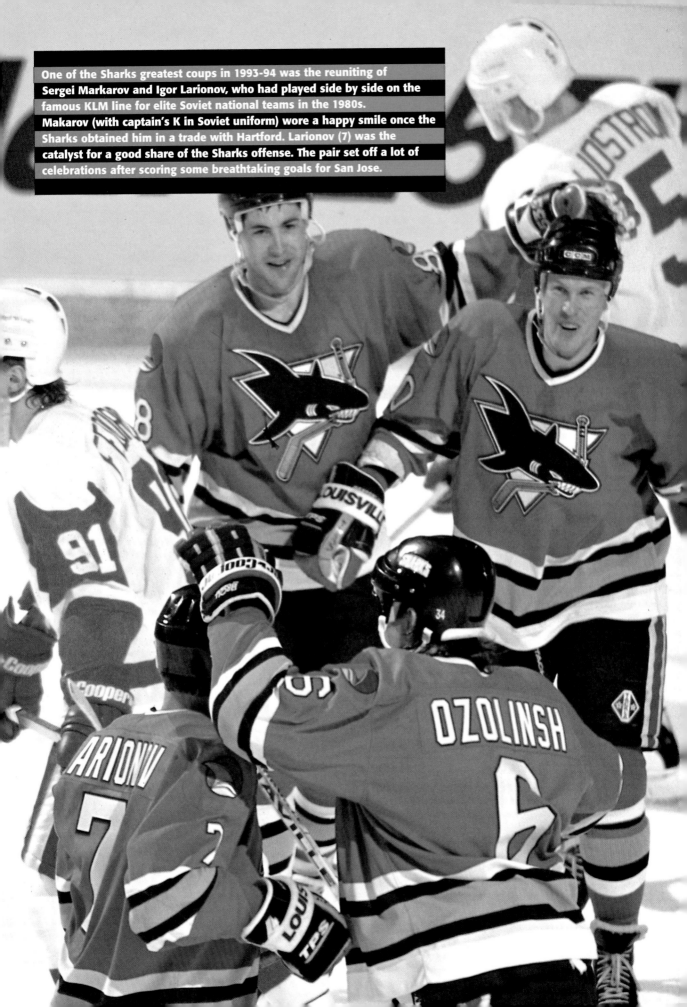

One of the Sharks greatest coups in 1993-94 was the reuniting of Sergei Markarov and Igor Larionov, who had played side by side on the famous KLM line for elite Soviet national teams in the 1980s. Makarov (with captain's K in Soviet uniform) wore a happy smile once the Sharks obtained him in a trade with Hartford. Larionov (7) was the catalyst for a good share of the Sharks offense. The pair set off a lot of celebrations after scoring some breathtaking goals for San Jose.

Russians, Swedes and Czechs. And by the way, there is a highly regarded prospect from Finland, Ville Peltonen, waiting in the wings.

San Jose also has an assistant coach, Vasily Tikhonov, who is the son of the legendary Soviet coach Viktor Tikhonov. The younger Tikhonov's wife even brought something to the happy mix—she teaches English to foreign players' wives to help everyone make an easier adjustment to life in North America.

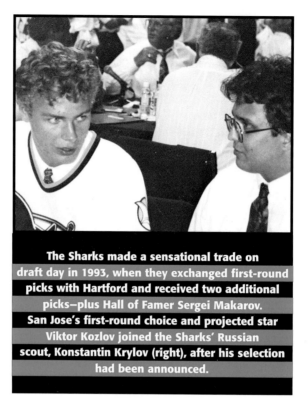

The Sharks made a sensational trade on draft day in 1993, when they exchanged first-round picks with Hartford and received two additional picks—plus Hall of Famer Sergei Makarov. San Jose's first-round choice and projected star Viktor Kozlov joined the Sharks' Russian scout, Konstantin Krylov (right), after his selection had been announced.

"We'll take being called The World's Team," Irbe said. "That just tells us management is happy to have players from all over the world. Everybody is so close, and that's unexpected. Other teams with some different nationalities have some problems, but for us, everything is settled."

Defenseman Jayson More, a Canadian, echoed that sentiment. "We've certainly come together as a close-knit family here," More said. "Sometimes it's tough to bring people of diverse backgrounds and get them to live together. I think it shows the character of this team."

Not so long ago, the entire NHL seemed to be almost exclusively a Canadian property. At least through the mid-1970s, the league's only flirtation beyond Canada's borders was exposure in the several United States cities where teams were based. Oh, there were a handful of Americans in the league—hardly any impact players—and as for Europeans, well, they were considered soft, patty-cake finesse skaters who could execute some pretty turns but who wouldn't absorb a body-check from a ballerina.

That bias took something of a beating when the brilliant, swooping, slick-passing Russians began to dominate international hockey. In the two decades leading up to the breakup of the Soviet Union, some of the world's best hockey teams came from behind the Iron Curtain.

Not only that, but the Soviets' success helped spur hockey booms in Sweden, Czechoslovakia, and Finland, other countries where kids always had been at home on frozen ponds.

Like it or not—and many Canadians didn't—the outlanders were bound to start arriving in the NHL. Not just fill-in players, either, but bona fide stars. Toronto's Swedish defenseman, Borje Salming, was one of the first breakthrough players in the 70s, but more were coming—including scoring wizard Jari Kurri.

And finally, when the former Soviet Union began to collapse and its incredible talent lode became available to NHL teams, the exodus was on. Russian Hall of Famers and future Sharks Sergei Makarov and Igor Larionov came over with several of their former teammates, and so did young phenoms like Buffalo's Alexander Mogilny and Detroit's Sergei Federov. Vancouver's "Russian Rocket," Pavel Bure, is probably the league's most exciting newcomer.

But one thing no NHL team had dared attempt until the Sharks dropped all thought of international barriers was the notion of putting a dozen or so non-Canadians on the same team and hoping that they not only could blend together, but that North American fans might accept them as easily as they would a gang of kids from Ontario or Manitoba.

SAN JOSE SHARKS

Even before they became a force on the ice, the Sharks took the NHL by storm with a dramatic logo and tremendously successful marketing push that saw Sharks merchandise selling wildly—not just in San Jose but around North America and even elsewhere in the world. The now-famous teal-and-black uniforms were unveiled in 1991 by (from left) club executive vice president Matt Levine, NHL Hall of Famer Gordie Howe, Sharks owner George Gund and president Art Savage.

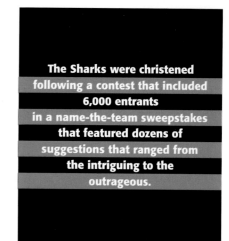

"I believe the multinational makeup of San Jose and our whole area made this the right place for it to take place," Sharks executive vice president Matt Levine said. "The entire Bay Area, the Santa Clara Valley—with Silicon Valley at the center—has been a mixture of cultures for quite awhile. It was a natural location for a hockey team representing several countries—a perfect fit."

Former San Jose mayor and current Sharks executive Tom McEnery wasn't surprised that his city embraced the polyglot Sharks. "The truth is that, because of Silicon Valley and so many of the huge international corporations that do business here, San Jose is probably better known around the world than it is in other parts of the United States," McEnery said.

"Even before the Sharks, San Jose meant more to someone in Europe or Asia than it probably did, say, in Alabama. In San Jose, we knew all along that accepting players from other countries wouldn't be a problem—a lot of our citizens and people they work with already had come from those same countries. Maybe a team with several Russians or Latvians would seem odd in Winnipeg or Calgary, but it's a perfectly comfortable situation in San Jose."

Selling the idea of the Sharks as The World's Team, however, is definitely a two-part deal. The gentlemen on the ice are only half of the equation.

Even before the Sharks' hockey staff could find winning players with such diverse roots, the franchise's marketing effort—one of most successful in the entire history of professional sports—had introduced the team, its spectacular logo and catchy color scheme to millions of potential fans.

The Sharks' marketing push began before the team played a single game and achieved such awesome results on a local, national and worldwide scale that one San Jose publication dubbed the whole thing, "Sharkie's Machine."

None of it happened by accident, either.

Levine had been a sports and entertainment consultant with dozens of high-profile clients for two decades by the time the Sharks approached him in 1990 and asked for help in re-launching hockey in the Bay Area—where it had failed dismally in the 1970s.

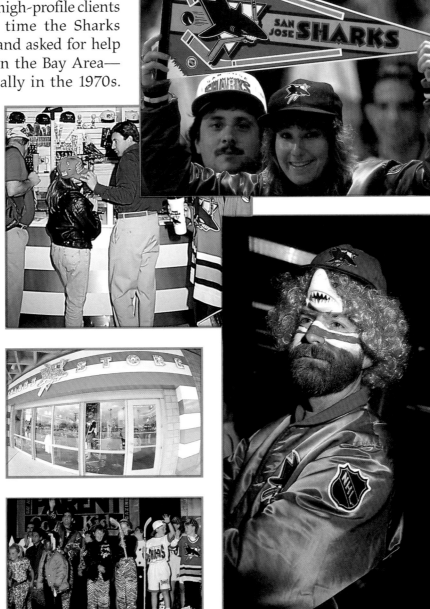

Levine, a scholarly sort who is almost the direct opposite of the old stereotypical sports promoter, promptly went about systematically canvassing thousands of people throughout the Sharks' new territory.

He supervised audience audits, focus groups and individual interviews to see just how the locals would perceive this new hockey team—who they were, what they liked, what competed for their leisure time, what they'd buy and how much they could spend.

This was definitely new ground for the old-guard NHL, which for years had relied on rough-and-tumble, bloodbath hockey and hoped to peddle it mainly to blue-collar patrons in the older, industrial cities where the sport traditionally had been based.

What Levine discovered was that times had changed, that fans of the 1990s wanted end-to-end action instead of Friday-night fisticuffs disguised as hockey. He found a potentially high-income audience that wanted family entertainment for its sports dollars—and in which women would play a startlingly large role.

The Sharks, in other words, were going against hockey's oldest maxim. They were headed toward upward mobility on every level.

"It's not a beer-swilling, epithet-throwing crowd that dominates the place," Levine said of the typical audience that has followed the Sharks from their first season in the Cow Palace into the glamorous new San Jose Arena. "Nearly a quarter of the fans have average yearly incomes in excess of $100,000. All the amenities are geared toward upscale service, upscale food, upscale security and attention to family atmosphere that's more friendly. Hockey games used to be an 80 percent male audience. Now at a Sharks game,

The Sharks' popularity has reached a point that some unusual products are turning into hot sellers, including S.J. Sharkie's wine.

As the house lights went out, spotlights lit up the sharkhead and the players skated out of the jaws to loud cheers and music. Talk about a great pregame show.

"My wife was very impressed with this trip. She loved the San Jose Arena and the way it catered to fans. Most of all, she was amazed at how friendly and courteous the staff was. It was a far cry from the teams east of the Mississippi."

The Sharks' approach—family entertainment, relentless civic activities, trendy uniforms and all-out merchandising of this appealing paraphernalia—brought immediate financial dividends. More than $125 million worth of Sharks goodies, from caps to keychains, were sold at retail in the Sharks first season, a staggering figure that easily topped the NHL (it represented 25 percent of the league's total) and helped make the team popular in places where no one could even name a single Sharks player. *Fortune* magazine did a study that proclaimed the Sharks had outsold every professional team except Michael Jordan's Chicago Bulls during those Cow Palace days.

All this from a team that was two years away from its first respectable season on the ice.

The NHL brass, which coincidentally was trying to change hockey's image by curbing brawls and promoting its newer, swift-skating stars, found itself utterly delighted by the Sharks' success.

"They've done a phenomenal job," said Fred Scalera, vice president of licensing for NHL Enterprises Inc. "They were the first new team in our recent expansion, and they helped bring the league into modern times. From soup to nuts, they did a great job. San Jose really helped lead the fashion charge. We know damn well a lot of Sharks merchandise is not being bought by avid hockey fans."

Perhaps the most telling compliment of all came two years after the Sharks debut, when the Disney-owned Mighty Ducks of

you're talking about 40 percent women. That changes the whole nature of the crowd. Instead of a game being like going out to a bar with your buddies, it's an entirely different experience."

Robert Wimmer, a Detroit-based columnist for *Sports Collectors Digest* and incurable hockey fan, decided to see for himself what all the fuss was about and took his wife on a trip to San Jose. The Wimmers were wowed.

"When the game was ready to start," Wimmer wrote, "the Sharks put on a great pre-program show utilizing multimedia techniques. My favorite was watching the huge shark's head come down from the ceiling...

"As the players got ready to come on the ice for the game, the shark's eyes started to blink red, then the mouth started to smoke.

Anaheim entered the league. Here was the mightiest marketing giant of all, with movies to showcase its nickname, hundreds of retail outlets throughout the world and those giant theme parks in which to peddle Ducks hockey merchandise—and it's just a fact that the Disney folks simply followed the Sharks' blueprint while leaping to the top of the sales chart for 1993-94.

Mighty Ducks executive Tony Taveras publicly has downplayed the Sharks' influence—what else would you expect from Disney's mega-mindset?—but he admitted, "One thing the Sharks did do was wake up everyone else in the league. We realize we can make some money off all this now."

While the Ducks and their massive merchandising juggernaut have surpassed the Sharks in paraphernalia purchases, San Jose's dramatic logo remains No. 1 in hockey—and presumably, in all pro sports. That's a fact: *The Hockey News* reported a study done by MBL-BBDO of Toronto, Canada's largest advertising firm. The company studied all 26 NHL logos on the basis of colors, design and team logo, and declared the Sharks' was best of all.

Michael McLaughlin, the ad company's creative director, explained that the Sharks' logo was tops because it's a perfect fit, tying in an aggressive central image with a novel color combination and a hostile name.

Levine and his lieutenants in the Sharks' marketing brain trust had taken no chances when they were fiddling with nicknames, logos and uniform designs. As with everything else, they did their homework.

The Sharks chose teal as their basic color only after Levine contacted several upscale mail-order catalog companies—Nieman-Marcus, J Crew, L.L. Bean, Bloomingdale's and mega-sports apparel licensee, Starter—to find out what schemes were most impressive. As Levine put it, "We wanted a color with legs for the 90s." The black was added because it was a natural match, it looked sharp with the basic teal uniform and it appealed to male buyers.

No outpost is too remote for The World's Team.
One fan in Antarctica put on formal attire
—with proper ballcap—to show his allegiance.

Levine was even picky about the shade of teal—he didn't want something with green in it. Eventually, the Sharks settled for a shade graphic designers know as Pantone 3145 and promptly gave it a name: Pacific teal. "Basically, we invented that name just because we wanted something with a local flavor," Levine said with a chuckle.

As for the Sharks' nickname, well, the public got involved in that. After the franchise had been granted and everyone in the Bay Area knew hockey was coming back—though San Jose hadn't yet been chosen as its official home—Levine supervised a gigantic Name-the-Team sweepstakes that drew nearly 2,300 suggestions from 6,000 people in 40 states and every Canadian province across North America, and even one from Genoa, Italy.

The Sharks still keep a copy of the entire

"You've heard of Canada's Team, America's Team. Our goal is to become The World's Team."

—*Chuck Grillo*

The Sharks are the most popular team in Russia because of players like Sergei Makarov and Igor Larionov. But American fans visiting cities like Moscow are also welcome to join in, as Eric Sanders of Walnut Creek demonstrated with the Kremlin in the background.

list of names around the office. It's great reading for a rainy day.

Can you imagine Arturs Irbe in goal for the San Jose Anacondas? How about the Bay O'Wolves? Or Barnacles? Some entrants just had to be spoofing, like the ones who suggested the team be called the Bart Simpsons, or the Cisco Kids, or City's Nitty Gritty. Would you still love these guys if they were the San Jose Fighting Pig Cats, or the Dead Dudes, or Frostbite? Jabberwocks? Or maybe the Icemen Cometh?

There were even some folks who thought the Valley's computer image ought to be incorporated—San Jose Hard Disks, for instance. Probecards. Semi-conductors. Silicon Chips. Disk Drives. Fighting Computer Salesmen. And so forth.

Eliminated early: Puck & Duck, Spineless Worms, Thugs, Swizzle Sticks, Vagrants, Surf Dudes, Yodeling Yams, Aurora Borealis, Bounced Checks, Bud Lite, Brain Patrol, Cansecos and hundreds more.

"The world comes together with our team better than the way the rest of the world has come together."

—George Gund

they fiddled with all sorts of possibilities. Eventually, it was decided that the shark should be black, with three gills (no such shark exists in nature) and that the background be a triangle to represent San Jose, San Francisco and Oakland —the Bay Area's three major cities.

For a time, Sharks executives weren't positive the league would accept the new logo. They feared it was just a bit too aggressive, particularly with the NHL making such an attempt at softening its rough-and-tumble image. Eventually, the design was approved, though Levine recalled one former league official saying that, while he liked Sharks' color scheme, he didn't think that logo would go anyplace at all.

Well...

Once the entire marketing package was in place, the Sharks promptly began selling it like crazy—and discovered that they'd struck gold. Same thing with the philosophy of family entertainment and upscale amenities in a show biz atmosphere for home games.

Not surprisingly, Sharks was one of the most popular entries, and it was one of the finalists almost immediately. "We wanted a one-syllable nickname to go with the three syllables of San Jose," Levine said. "One of the things that pushed us toward Sharks was that we did some research, and discovered that there was an area just off the Pacific Coast between San Francisco and San Jose called the 'Red Triangle,' which is home to seven different species of shark."

So Sharks it was, and thus the next item was designing the logo which now has become so famous around the world. Levine put a team of artists on the project, and

Yes, there was some resentment directed at the Sharks' overall philosophy from old-line hockey quarters. Grumpy fans from eastern cities, particularly in Canada, groused about the fancy-pants teal uniforms—on a California team, no less. Author Stan Fischler, a traditionalist in every sense of the word, decried the league's softer stance, its sudden aversion to brawling, its new love for the American Sunbelt and just about everything else that didn't remind him of 1950s hockey.

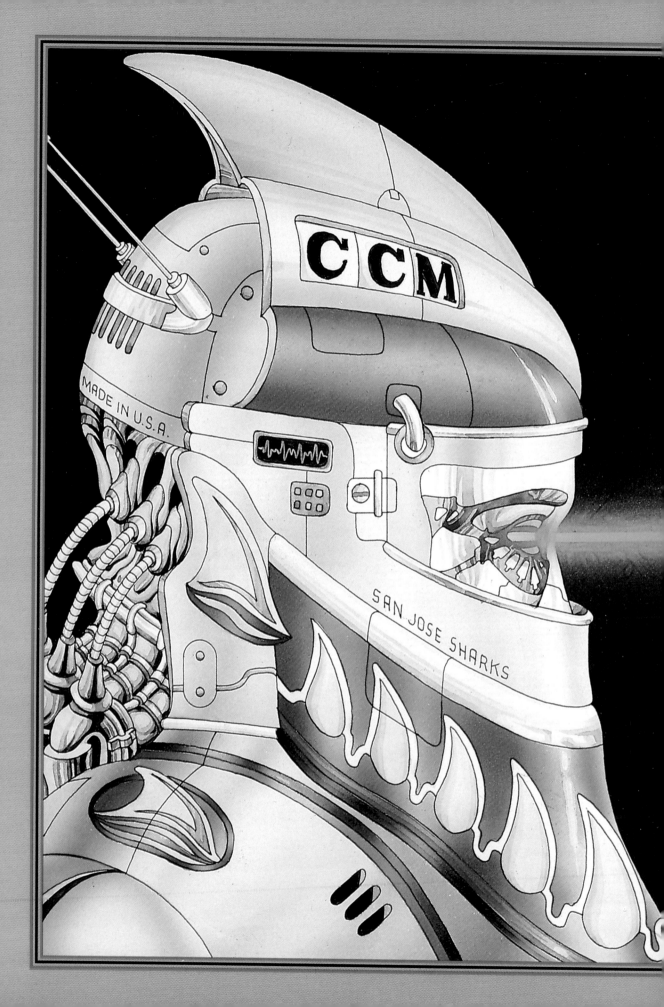

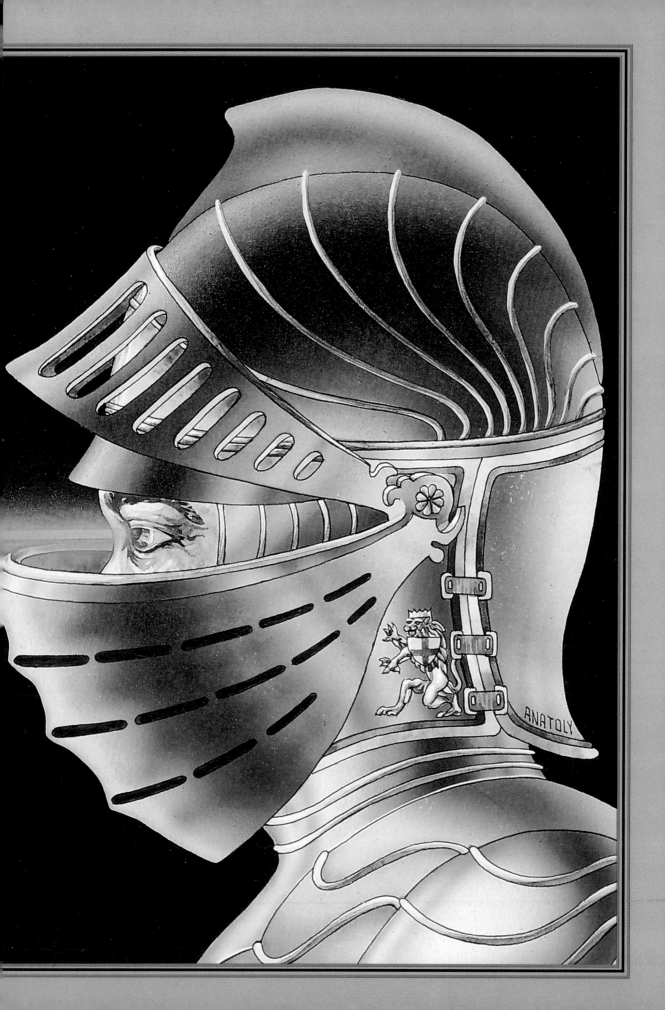

Gina Staffieny of San Jose made sure the Sharks were represented right at the center of the world they hope to conquer.

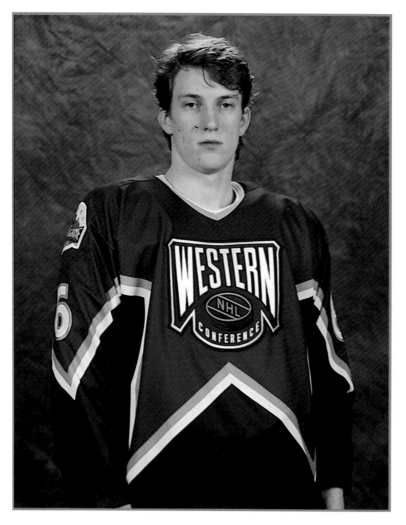

The Sharks just smiled.

"A lot of writers get to a certain age and pine for days of yore," Levine observed. "It's our mission in the sports and entertainment industry to create constructive change. The world is changing, and we can't just stand still or it's going to pass us by. There is indeed a segment of people out there who like hockey the way it was. But they are becoming a smaller and smaller segment of the whole.

"It's important to remember, though, that we were different not just for our own sake. Our objective was not just to be different, but innovative, and the NHL was very supportive. We have the greatest respect for the traditions of hockey. As (commissioner) Gary Bettman is demonstrating, you can pay tribute to the original six teams and their traditions, and still do what's best for the future of the sport.

"Whatever we do, we want to ask: Do the Sharks represent the NHL and hockey well in North America and around the world? Do people like it?

"It seems like the answer is a resounding yes."

For a franchise that yearned someday to become The World's Team, you could hardly ask for a more auspicious start. Finding players good enough to win games would have come down the road, though everyone fervently hoped success on the scoreboard might be measured in seasons instead of decades.

Who could have imagined that the hockey team—the guys on the ice trying to match all that excitement in the seats and at the souvenir shops—would catch up with its glitzy image in just three short years?

And needless to say, the Sharks never could have pulled it off unless they'd turned up talent from all parts of the compass—with two talented Latvians landing in the 1994 All-Star game, with a pair of remarkable Russians reunited for a last hurrah, with a Swedish scorer snatched via trade just 13 games from the end of the season?

"Sometimes you hear things in Canada about these guys—Swedes, for instance—not having heart," Grillo said. "Well, you can't buy passion. You have to draft it, and we drafted Ulf Dahlen when I was in the New York Rangers organization. We knew the passion we were getting when we made the trade for Ulf near the end of the year. We knew."

Forgive Gund, Lombardi, Grillo, Constantine and all those Sharks scouts and coaches if they give thanks every day for the good sense to keeping looking all over the world.

"You start with Irbe in goal," Lombardi said. "A couple of years ago, he was a raw kid with talent who was new to this country, struggling to get comfortable speaking English, still learning the North American game. Now he's the guy who can keep us in games night after night, and for a team that's trying to develop piece by piece, a great goalie is something straight from heaven.

"Then think about Larionov and Makarov, and what they brought to us. Our fans went from seeing a team the year before that had trouble making three passes in a row to watching two of the best players hockey has ever seen—back together, sometimes looking almost magical.

"I like to say that Wayne Gretzky gave birth to hockey to Northern California with the success he had down in Los Angeles, then Larionov and Makarov mothered it. We'll be forever indebted to them."

The Sharks heard all the

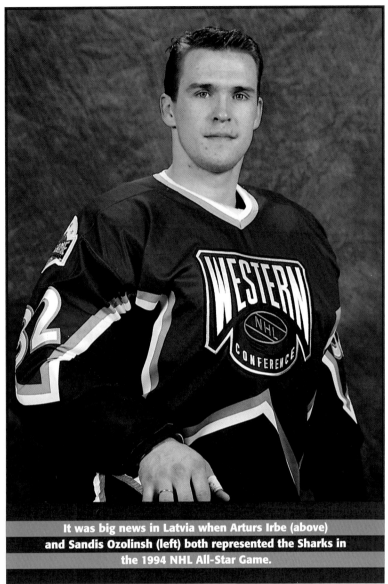

It was big news in Latvia when Arturs Irbe (above) and Sandis Ozolinsh (left) both represented the Sharks in the 1994 NHL All-Star Game.

sniping from north of the border when they threw all these Latvians and Russians and Swedes and Vlasty Kroupa—an 18-year-old Czech defenseman—into a melting pot and started inching toward the playoffs. The old-liners in Canada turned up their noses, which is why, no matter what they said, the Sharks desperately wanted their second-round playoff opponent to be Toronto.

"I won't deny it," Lombardi said. "We dreamed of going to Toronto, right into the heart of hockey country, to the center of hockey in Canada, to prove that we could play the game. It would have been spectacular to win that series with the Leafs, but just playing it the way we did,

we made our statement. Just because we had guys from different countries didn't mean we lacked character, and Toronto found that out."

Maple Leafs captain Wendel Clark agreed.

"If (Johan) Garpenlov's shot goes in, there's no Game Seven," Clark said. "If Ozolinsh scores on his opportunity, there's no Game Seven. If my pass in overtime doesn't bounce off the skate of their defenseman right to Mike Gartner, there's no Game Seven. Those guys never died."

It should not be a surprise to Sharks fans, then, that Gund, Lombardi, Grillo, scouting coordinator Joe Will and everyone else in the hockey side of the organization continues to

There won't be any letup in the search for foreign-born talent. The Sharks have high hopes for Czech-born defenseman Michal Sykora.

roam the world in search of talent. The Sharks insist they're as interested in Canadian prospects as anybody else—their first-round draft choice in 1994 was Jeff Friesen of Meadow Lake, Saskatchewan—but they just simply refuse to have tunnel vision.

"A lot of people think our foundation is all European," Grillo said, "and that's the wrong perception. We spend a lot of time and effort and money scouting Canadian and American players. The reality is that we've just blended that with an effort overseas that a lot of teams haven't.

"A good share of the NHL is still Canadian, and some people in it only think Canadian. There's still a bias there. The difference is that we're unbiased, so when we put together our scouting lists, we're basing decisions on good players and good people instead of where they're from. The result is that, when our turn comes up, some very good European players are still available that wouldn't be if the other teams' lists weren't biased toward Canadians.

"That's not our problem. It's their problem."

The Sharks also have a couple of huge advantages in scouting and signing Europeans that other clubs can only envy. One is their sophisticated computerization, which serves to collate information from scouts and allows almost instantaneous

One thing that makes Sharks executives bristle is the suggestion that their scouting is tilted primarily overseas. Instead, they say, it merely includes the whole world on an equal basis. San Jose chose Jeff Friesen of Meadow Lake, Saskatchewan, in the first round of the 1994 draft.

cross-checking of prospects—whether they're from downtown Toronto or some timber town in the Russian outback.

Scouting coordinator Will developed a computer program that has logged 15,000 prospects from around the world into its data base. The system works—in the time Grillo, Will and Company have been together in Minnesota and now San Jose, they've averaged four successful draft selections per year. The league average is 1.6. "I'm extremely proud of our dedicated staff," says Grillo.

"We've had an offer of $3 million to buy an exclusive program and $300,000 to share one with others," Grillo said of the Sharks' computer advantage. "We didn't even think about taking it."

And then there's perhaps the biggest advantage of them all.

"George Gund deserves a tremendous amount of credit," Grillo said. "There just isn't any other owner like him. He's just loved all over the hockey world. He can go anywhere, from Scandinavia to Russia or anyplace else, and people love him. They know what he represents. He's a master of setting others up to succeed. He is a very special human being.

"Players know that, too. Every single European player wants to play for the San Jose Sharks."

Lombardi and Grillo can tell endless stories of Gund hopping onto his airplane—the one with the Sharks logo on the side—and zooming off to watch some prospect play, often on a moment's notice and just as often in some remote

corner of the globe.

"He (Gund) will take his plane and go scout at a tournament in Mexico City," Grillo said. "I remember one trip, we had some players we wanted to see, and we went from Prague to Finland, to Moscow and back to Prague—one day each. No way we could have done anything like that on a commercial plane. George Gund is so unbelievable, it's scary.

"One time, George got us into Riga at a time when there was still trouble with the Russian troops being there. We landed and there were soldiers with machine guns all

Club owner George Gund (center, with Sharks jacket) has made no secret that he's willing to travel far and wide as part of the team's search for players. At this press conference in Riga, Latvia, Gund and other club officials were discussing a promising defenseman they'd just scouted —future San Jose star Sandis Ozolinsh.

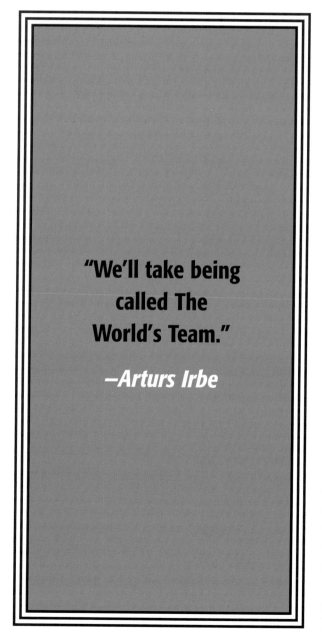

"We'll take being called The World's Team."

—*Arturs Irbe*

around, and we didn't even have passports. George just dropped the plane right down, and told somebody that we had to go to the hockey rink. Somehow, we went to the game and when we got back to our hotel, we had passports. Nobody but George Gund could have done that."

If Sharks executives sometimes sound as though they're on a faster track than other teams in the areas of scouting and development—in Europe and everywhere else—it's simply because they believe it.

"Nobody's going to work harder than we are. We now have a template in place with real standards for our young players. If there's talent out there, we can find it," Grillo said. "Dean knows how to put it together, and we all know Kevin Constantine can coach it. We're prepared, we're organized, and we're totally committed because we love what we're doing. Don't doubt that we'll succeed.

"The World's Team. You have to like the sound of it, because it really fits the San Jose Sharks."

128

Sharks scouting supervisor Tim Burke (left) and Chuck Grillo met some young fans on a trip to Stockholm, Sweden, in 1993.

The Sharks plan to keep up with their globe-trotting talent hunt. Player personnel chief Chuck Grillo (left) and Russian-born assistant coach Vasily Tikhonov stepped off owner George Gund's teal-and-black private plane in Peri, Finland.

Mania at The Tank: 6,000 to 10,000 playoff-crazed fans watched live action on the arena video screens.

FIVE

Hockey Heaven

The trick is in always remembering where you've been.

It's about the legacy of Dean Evason and Brian Hayward and Paul Fenton. Craig Coxe and Perry Berezan. Kelly Kisio and Wayne Presley and Neil Wilkinson. Bob McGill and Robin Bawa and, yes, coach George Kingston and the first general manager, Jack Ferreira. It's recalling that bona fide All-Star Doug Wilson came along to midwife an infant team at the end of his brilliant career.

And it's most certainly about keeping a hat tipped forever toward that first wave of screaming teal-covered fans who invented The Chomp and refused to lose faith during so many long, long nights at the Cow Palace.

The Sharks are home now in a spectacular new arena. They're heroes in a city that has burst into the spotlight after years of dozing among the orchards and being known mostly as that oversized fruit-and-vegetable stand an hour south of San Francisco.

Suddenly, the Sharks are a national phenomenon.

On a football show during October of 1994, ESPN host Chris Berman was talking about the NFL's use of "throwback" uniforms as, on certain weekends, teams were wearing togs from some distant season. Berman was particularly enthralled by the San Diego Chargers' powder-blue jerseys from 1961, and suggested that people soon would be out buying the Chargers' old shirts by the thousands. "Before long, they'll be as hot as the San Jose Sharks," Berman said.

Point taken: San Jose's franchise has heated up enough to melt its own shimmering ice.

You can find a

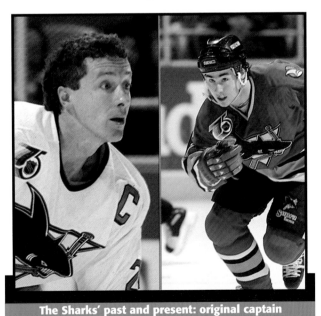

The Sharks' past and present: original captain Doug Wilson (left) represented the team's growing stages during its first two seasons, while winger Pat Falloon—San Jose's first-ever selection in the entry draft—hopes someday soon to carry the Stanley Cup.

tough and clever coach in charge, savvy veterans and emerging stars up and down the roster, one serious run through the Stanley Cup playoffs already in the sack. Luxury boxes are top-dollar items, tickets are precious as diamonds and the San Jose Sharks clearly have become an organization on the bullet train upward.

But the only way to appreciate the present is to keep a carefully framed mental picture of the past.

"The only way we can look at it is the record. It must have been hell to go through it," said center Todd Elik, one of the newcomers who rang up 25 goals and helped the Sharks snap things around in their remarkable playoff season.

"It would be hard for somebody who wasn't here (in 1992-93, when the Sharks were defeated 71 times) to understand all we went through, the feelings you had while you were losing 17 in a row," said rugged winger Jeff Odgers, who has been in the San Jose organization from the beginning — from the club's IHL affiliate in Kansas City right through the miracle of '94. "The guys who have been around from the start can appreciate what's happened, and how it feels."

Pardon the Sharks their smiles, but it feels just fine.

It's been repeated over and over that the Sharks' 58-point improvement in 1993-94 marked the greatest turnaround in NHL history, but it's also worth noting that San Jose became the first team since the 1975 Islanders to advance past the first round in a playoff debut. And by the way, that Islanders team — like the Sharks — was structured to survive far down the road by its own scouting and development wits, which it did by going on to win four Stanley Cup titles. The Sharks are planning to follow a similar blueprint.

Whatever happens on the ice, however, San Jose will never be the same.

Oh, there are plenty of people who think the 1993-94 dream season was a once-in-a-

"It would be hard for somebody who wasn't here (in 1992-93, when the Sharks were defeated 71 times) to understand all we went through, the feelings you had while you were losing 17 in a row."

—Jeff Odgers

Hockey fever has gripped San Jose so powerfully that city buses were repainted and a Sharks motif was added.

lifetime experience, that the city of San Jose and all those Bay Area fans doing The Chomp soon enough will slip back to a more sensible reality.

San Jose native Gary Radnich, an area radio and TV sports personality, is one of the cold-water tossers. "Five years from now, maybe when the Sharks do win a Stanley Cup, we'll be hardened and conditioned to having pro hockey," Radnich said. "This is as great as it's ever going to be. The true test

for San Jose hockey fans will be next year or the year after, when they're not the No. 1 story in hockey, and when they're playing Winnipeg or Ottawa on a Wednesday night and nothing's at stake."

Mark Purdy, former San Jose sports editor who watched the whole thing fall into place, begged to disagree.

"I hear there is a feeling this love affair between the Sharks and San Jose won't ever be as sweet as this spring," Purdy wrote

"Before long,
they'll be as
hot as the
San Jose
Sharks."

—*Chris Berman*

during the '94 playoff drama. "That it won't ever feel this way again, because this is the first time.

"I'm betting that's wrong. The point is, San Jose now has a chance to have it happen once more, because the Sharks will be there. And if they reach the Stanley Cup finals in 2002, how won't it feel as good? In baseball, the Giants went 27 years between World Series appearances. When they finally returned in 1989, I heard no Giants'

fans say, 'Gee, this only feels pretty nice, because it doesn't match the emotion I felt in 1962.'"

As Purdy pointed out, the key is that the Sharks are here. San Jose never has had its own major-league team — despite a couple of false romances with the Giants — and who's to say the city can't go right on enjoying the hockey experience?

Sure, the first-blush aspect of it all should wear off, but you actually might make the

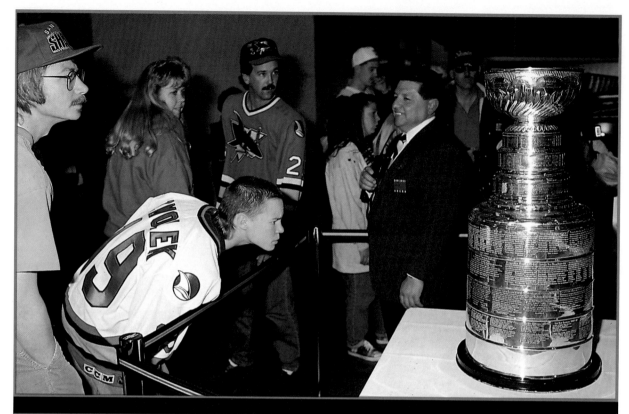
Yes, that's the real Stanley Cup. Sharks fans have admired it up close, and before long they'd like to bring it to San Jose.

case that the relationship between the Sharks and their hometown will get even stronger as the citizenry learns more and more about the game and its stars.

On the ice, there is every reason to believe the Sharks will provide plenty of thrills for their fans through the years. A feature story in *Hockey Stars Presents* about the team's Cinderella run in the '94 playoffs wrapped up this way:

"They were like the creature in *Jaws*, the man-eating shark that wouldn't go away. The Leafs, like the boat Jaws ate, were left half-eaten and in pieces. The scavenger Canucks swallowed what was left.

"But just when you thought it was safe to go back onto the ice...remember, there was a *Jaws II*."

The folks charged with keeping the Sharks competitive won't be sitting around on the laurels of one surprisingly successful season. No way. Chuck Grillo, the man who missed most of the Sharks' playoff games because he

was off hunting talent in far-flung spots, sent an E-mail to the team prior to the Toronto series, and Constantine read it to his players. Grillo's no-nonsense message was that he wasn't looking for one Stanley Cup, but several. "When you become a dynasty," Grillo wrote, "then you can smile."

Now that's what you call commitment to the future.

However the Sharks fare in the NHL standings from season to season, though, one thing is certain: The organization is doing everything possible to keep this hockey excitement from being some passing fancy in their hometown.

Consider the Sharks & Parks program, for example, which soon should have about 40,000 girls and boys involved in street hockey. The NHL liked that idea so much that, with support from Nike, several other teams in the U.S. and Canada have begun adopting it. And then there's the Break the Ice program, in which San Jose-area companies are invited to have employees learn to skate and how-to-stick handle at group functions. S.J. Sharkie, the team's popular mascot, turns up again and again around the area — not just to boost the Sharks' image but to show that the franchise is dedicated to participating in civic affairs. For example, The Sharks Foundation directs funding toward regional youth and education beneficiaries.

"One of our goals from the beginning was to establish a bond between the Sharks and our community," club president Art Savage said. "We want the ties to be strong. We don't want to just play hockey and sell tickets. Our players and coaches and staff will always be out there in public, involved in worthwhile projects and helping make sure this is a two-way relationship."

It's working: Coach Kevin Constantine was delighted to hear from several local schools. "I've gotten letters from kindergarten teachers saying they use the Sharks as an example of never quitting, never stop trying," Constantine said.

Greg Jamison, the Sharks chief operating officer, joined the club in 1993 after 13 years in the NBA. Among other duties, he was charged with making sure hockey endures with something more than a "curiosity" effect on San Jose.

"Sometimes things are novelties and wear off quickly," Jamison said. "Sometimes they take hold, and we think this has taken hold. The fact that it is San Jose's and Santa Clara County's (team) is a point of pride. Plus the fact that the arena is in the city, right downtown, lends itself to a strong sense of loyalty.

"It was tough winning only 11 games last year, so this year (1993-94) has been even more fun. I see people come out for the first time and like it. As one person told me, he brought somebody to a game, showed them how the blue line works, explained offside, and that's all you really need.

"We're looking to bring not only good hockey, but a flair to the presentation. The NHL puts

Dean Lombardi, the Sharks director of hockey operations, made the moves that catapulted the team into the playoffs in 1993-94, but Lombardi and his colleagues refuse to be satisfied. They have higher goals.

a good, strong product on the ice from the entertainment standpoint. We need to continue to entertain, but the entertainment is never meant to overshadow the product. Sports marketing sometimes gets away from that. We want to enhance the product. We want people to say, 'I went to watch the San Jose Sharks play a hockey game. While I was there, they gave away this and that and I really had a good time.'"

By the end of the 1993-94 season, there already was evidence that one type of bond was being formed: Fans knew more about hockey and its players.

"At the beginning, when I came here, you could go out and not be recognized," winger Gaetan Duchesne said. "Now, everywhere you go, at least one person recognizes you. It's nice. You can see we made a difference here, and people are

DEC CALIF

SJS

ORNIA CA 91
M1572685
HARX

starting to really like hockey now."

Constantine is famous for his work ethic, but even Kevin needs to get away — at least for a little while. So after the '94 playoffs had run their course, Constantine and his wife, Peggy, took off for a short hideaway vacation in Hawaii.

Except for the beaches, they might as well have been standing outside San Jose Arena. "On the first day we were in the islands," Constantine said, "we counted 23 people who recognized me and stopped to ask about the season. The only reason we started counting was that it was so surprising, we really began thinking it was funny.

"I don't consider myself a celebrity. I still get nervous and antsy just thinking about having a conversation with somebody like (Oakland A's manager) Tony La Russa. But the way the Sharks took hold in San Jose, I guess I have to get used to it. Toward the end of last season, it was difficult to go

anywhere without being recognized. Isn't that something?"

Perhaps not, when you put the city of San Jose into the equation.

This is a community which, like the Sharks, truly can enjoy its burst into the limelight because the locals have no trouble remembering the slights of the past.

"We've had all kinds of great things going on in San Jose and throughout the Valley for some time — the revitalization of downtown, new industries, the Children's Discovery Museum, the Technology Center of Silicon Valley, great new hotels, an expansion of the art museum — but people outside the area still kind of looked at us like a farm town where there's nothing to do," said former mayor Tom McEnery.

"San Jose got used to being put down. It wasn't fair, especially in recent years, but nobody came around to notice what had changed. But then when the arena was

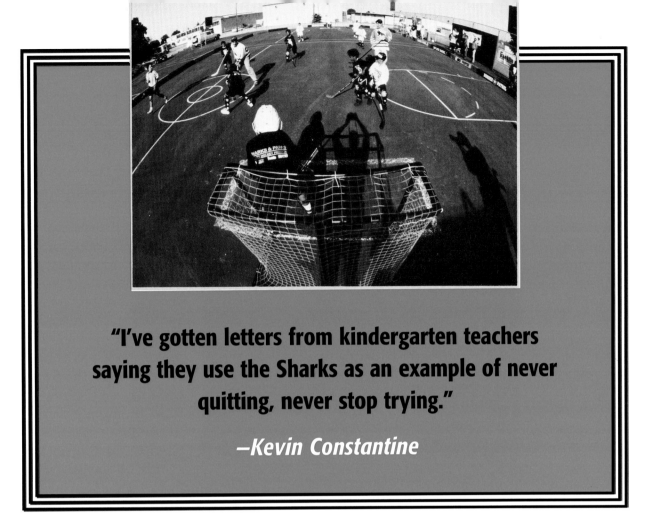

"I've gotten letters from kindergarten teachers saying they use the Sharks as an example of never quitting, never stop trying."

–Kevin Constantine

built, and all of a sudden Luciano Pavarotti and Barbra Streisand are in town, and the Sharks take off, everyone seemed to discover us all at once.

"And they liked what they found."

Dean Munro, who was one of McEnery's chief lieutenants in the difficult battle to get the arena initiative approved by voters in 1988, doesn't mince words about what effect the building and the Sharks have had on San Jose. "The arena and the hockey team have put us on the map," Munro said.

Such publicity means a lot to San Jose, which forever has suffered in the shadow of its Bay Area neighbors — especially the glamour of San Francisco, just an hour to the north.

"The Sharks puts us up there in the big leagues, it's just that simple," said Steve Tedesco, San Jose's Chamber of Commerce chief. "It's the marquee name. San Francisco isn't a world-class city because of the Giants and 49ers. It's a big city, a physically impressive city. But the Sharks put us in the same rink."

Or as public relations consultant Shari Boxer described the Sharks' arrival: "It legitimizes San Jose. It's like we're one of you guys."

There is also little doubt that the Sharks' ascent has meant a financial windfall for San Jose and its merchants in general, and for downtown in particular. "Count the teal jerseys and multiply by 50 bucks every time there's a home game," Tedesco joked. "There's serious money changing hands."

McEnery puts the fiscal picture into a far wider perspective. "National exposure is something that's almost invaluable," he said. "This sort of thing can really mean big money to the city's bottom line. You're talking about what amounts to free advertising, the type a city couldn't buy if it tried. This was like catching lightning in a

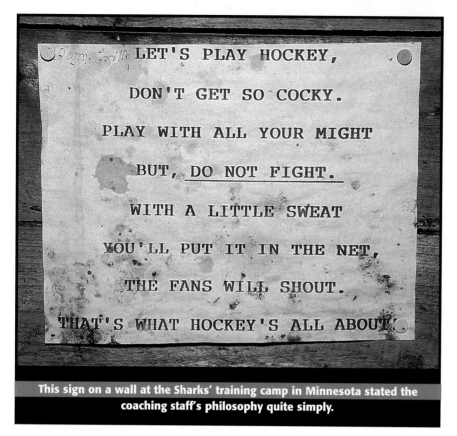

LET'S PLAY HOCKEY,

DON'T GET SO COCKY.

PLAY WITH ALL YOUR MIGHT

BUT, DO NOT FIGHT.

WITH A LITTLE SWEAT

YOU'LL PUT IT IN THE NET,

THE FANS WILL SHOUT.

THAT'S WHAT HOCKEY'S ALL ABOUT.

This sign on a wall at the Sharks' training camp in Minnesota stated the coaching staff's philosophy quite simply.

this was the right kind of place for hockey to take off. This team was really suited for the Silicon Valley.

"But far more important than that was the fact that people had something of their own, to be proud of their own team, of San Jose having the best."

Tom Tutko, a sports psychologist and professor at San Jose State University, suspects there is another reason the Sharks became so popular in the Santa Clara Valley. "If you were to ask the average person to name three of the Sharks, they probably couldn't," Tutko said. "These are not egomaniacal people like Charles Barkley. They're just guys who worked hard and had success — and we're not paying them $10 million each. I would hope the love affair would endure."

None of these San Jose movers and shakers — from McEnery to Munro to Tedesco to current mayor Susan Hammer — have been even slightly surprised at the downtown celebrations that accompany Sharks games. They reason that all those neat hotels and restaurants and refurbished little bistros already had changed the city's face, and a red-hot hockey team only put the icing on the cake.

Most San Jose residents have harbored a longtime resentment at the perception their city received in the pre-Sharks era, and many are willing to admit it.

"Maybe it was a little like bitterness," Tedesco said. "We know we've got a good city. We may even be a great city. We know we weren't recognized within the world, and that irritated the hell out of us."

But they're getting it now.

Listen to Marion Holt, president of the

bottle, with CBS coming to town, and *USA Today*, and *The New York Times*. They're all here, showing off San Jose. If you want to put a dollar value on what the Sharks have contributed to the city's image, you might start, honestly, with a billion dollars.

"That's how much it means to get the attention that comes with a major-league franchise, especially in a city that doesn't already have one."

Ironically, McEnery's first choice as a tenant for his dream arena was the Golden State Warriors. "I admit I was thinking about basketball when we first started planning the arena campaign," he said, "but it's turned out that hockey was the best possible choice. Here's a sport that is tremendously exciting — once you get involved, you fall hard — and it captures the imagination of kids and women. And as for what is essentially a foreign sport to American fans, we had a natural base for it.

"San Jose is kind of the world's valley. We've got people here who know a little bit of everything from nuclear fission to jai alai, so

Cover art for *Sharks Magazine* specially designed by Charles Schulz

153

The Sharks' arrival in San Jose has meant a boom in youth hockey for the entire area. The kids have gotten plenty of chances to skate between periods at Sharks games, too.

Coach Kevin Constantine and his wife, Peggy, have become two of San Jose's most popular residents.

San Jose Convention and Visitors Bureau: "I was on a business trip in Europe and saw highlights on television in Budapest of the Sharks' win (over Detroit in the first game of the playoffs). "It was in Hungarian, but you couldn't miss the color of the uniforms and the logo." In Paris, Holt found a headline in the *International Herald Tribune* which read: "Unsung Sharks a Polyglot Miracle."

One of the things which pleases Valley residents the most is that the success of the Sharks — and San Jose Arena — has come at the expense of San Francisco, where there has always been an air of smug superiority hanging over conversations that included its neighbor to the south.

San Jose not only has a hockey team making national headlines, but the city has snatched several prestigious events away from San Francisco and Oakland — a major tennis tournament, the national figure-skating championships and, lest anyone forget, the NHL All-Star Game. The celebrity migration south brings smiles to the faces of the long-silent majority in San Jose.

"We've been schlepping somewhere else for years to do things," said Vicki L. Herl, who manages a retail shopping pavilion in downtown San Jose. "We don't have any sympathy for them on that one."

In fact, demographic studies show that 63 percent of Sharks' patrons come from the Santa Clara Valley — but that leaves a very healthy 37 percent who are trekking in from somewhere else, including San Francisco and its environs.

Team mascot S.J. Sharkie has become a fixture around the San Jose area, and not just at games. S.J. Sharkie is used as one of the franchise's ambassadors for civic affairs, youth functions and other events.

> **"We know we've got a good city.
> We may even be a great city.
> We know we weren't recognized
> within the world, and that irritated
> the hell out of us."**
>
> *—Steve Tedesco,*
> **president, Chamber of Commerce**

"We invite them all to come down to see all San Jose has to offer," Mayor Hammer said. "If anybody thought there wasn't any there there, those people are welcome to visit our neighborhoods and enjoy our city."

Bottom line: The Sharks and their sparkling new arena have given San Jose a brighter overall image, civic pride, national and worldwide exposure — and the right, finally, for locals to swell out their chests and brag a little.

Everyone seems to have a favorite story, a particular moment or a significant event that stands out in this real-life fairy tale about how a city and hockey team could fall so hopelessly loopy over one another.

Perhaps McEnery's sums up the entire Sharks phenomenon in San Jose.

"One of the greatest scenes of all," he said, "was during the playoffs when the Sharks opened up the arena for fans who wanted to come and watch the games in Detroit and Toronto on the big video screens. I mean, people could have stayed home and seen the games in their own living rooms, but they wanted to be at the arena, being part of it all, enjoying the whole experience together.

"So there was this magnificent arena, with all the partying going on outside and the enthusiasm building up, and then there would be 10,000 people — dressed in teal, wearing Sharks hats, all kinds of crazy things — and they'd sit there and scream and cheer.

"Think about it: Thousands of fans, all hollering like mad and there's nothing in front of them but empty ice. What an experience. Seeing that was seeing our dream come true."

The dream that was a wisp so few years ago. The dream that became the San Jose Sharks.

Mayor Susan Hammer became a fanatic Sharks supporter along with everyone else. Hammer loved the team and the excitement it generated, but she also was gratified by the attention the Sharks brought to San Jose—particularly its revitalized downtown area.

1993-94 SHARKS &

ALL

GOO

Franklin SPORTS

The Sharks & Parks program has helped create thousands of young and enthusiastic street hockey players in San Jose. This Sharks-sponsored effort has been adopted by the NHL and several other teams plan to copy it.

RKS ALL-STAR STREET HOCKEY
RNAMENT
R CHAMPIONSHIP
JOSE ARENA
CK & GREAT HOCKEY!

SAN JOSE
SHARKS

KGO-TV 7
SAN FRANCISCO · OAKLAND · SAN JOSE

House
of
Engraving

There's never been anything like it in San Jose: Thousands of Sharks fans turned out at The Tank to watch road playoff games on the arena's video screens. They were hollering at empty ice, but nobody seemed to mind—it was too much fun.

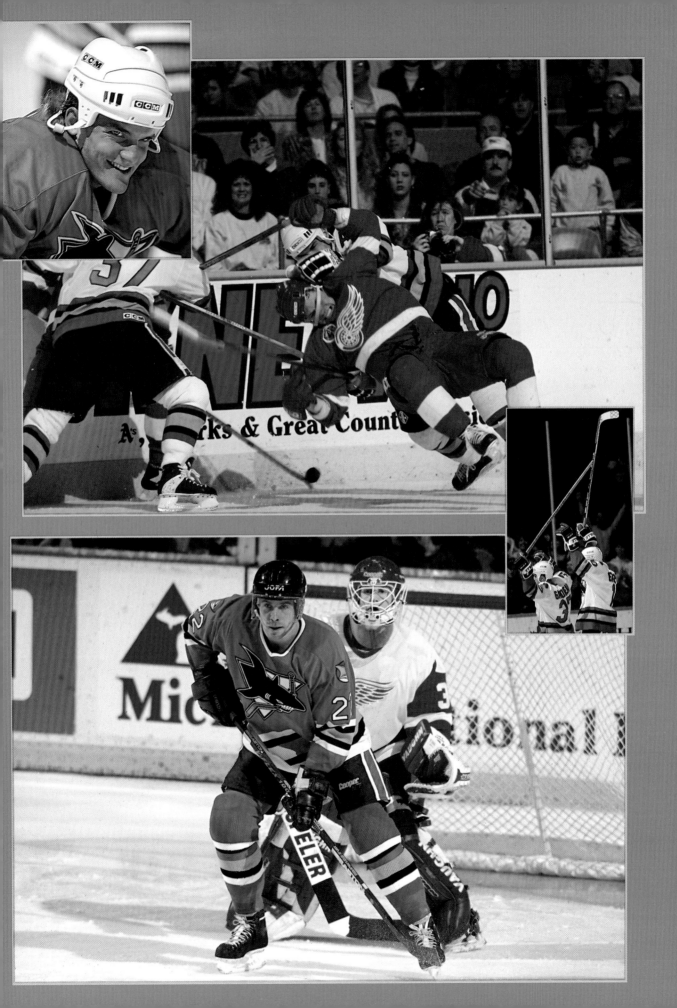

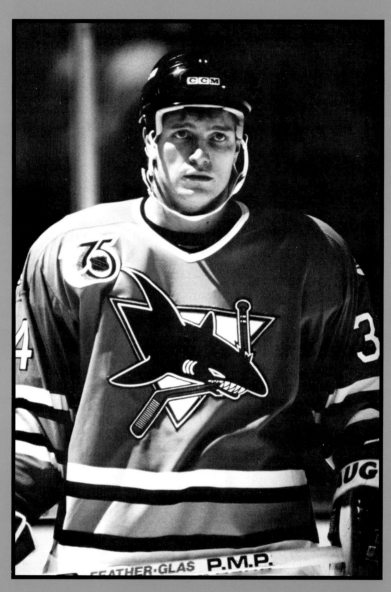

In Memory of Mike Colman